D0240550

TOTALLY
FLOUR-FREE
BAKING

TOTALLY
FLOUR-FREE
BAKING

DINAH ALISON

OVER 100 EASY FLOUR-FREE RECIPES
for low-starch breads, cakes, cookies, quiches, waffles and more

Avital Books

Published by Avital Books, PO Box 1871, Andover, Hampshire SP10 9AJ.

Text Copyright 2005 © Dinah Alison.

Photography Copyright 2005 © Dinah Alison.

The moral right of the author has been asserted.

All rights reserved. Without limiting the rights under copyright reserved above, no part of this publication may be reproduced, stored in or introduced into a retrieval system, or transmitted, in any form or by any means (electronic, mechanical, photocopying, recording or otherwise), without the prior written permission of the copyright owner of the book.

Designed by Carole McDonald, Butler and Tanner, Frome, Somerset.

Printed and bound by Butler and Tanner.

ISBN 0-9550702-0-1

Caution: These recipes contain nuts. As with all recipes, check before serving that all the ingredients are suitable for the intended recipient.

The author cannot verify that ingredients used are flour-free, or accept responsibility for changes in ingredient content. The use of branded products does not imply that the product is, or will remain, flour-free. It is up to the user to continually check that the ingredients used are suitable for the intended consumer.

ACKNOWLEDGEMENTS

I would particularly like to thank the following people who, wittingly or otherwise, have contributed to the making of this book.

My **Grandfather**, for telling me when I was little that cooking was elementary laboratory work. My **Mother**, for the timely interruption that sent me in a different direction during the experiments. My **Father**, who will now know that he's been eating nuts all along. **Christopher**, who proved repeatedly that the recipes can be made by non-cooks – and for his tireless tasting, excellent suggestions, endless editing and constant support. **Jeremy**, for constant encouragement and patient and tireless assistance with everything technological in my life. **Dodie**, for refocusing me and bringing balance to my life, always… **Audrey**, for willingly sacrificing her waistline during the tasting sessions, and her considered – and correct – suggestions for improvements to the recipes. **Angela**, for sending me in the right direction. **Tim**, for enthusiastic help, patient explanations, kindness and direction. **Carole**, for patience, persistence, tact and excellent translation of my ideas. **Nick**, for kind encouragement and photographic assistance. Everyone else at Butler and Tanner who took the time to explain how the printing process works, and ensured that this book looks as I imagined.

CONTENTS

Introduction   6

Notes   8

Useful Equipment   12

Breads   14

Cakes   30

Biscuits & Bars   68

Desserts & Sweet Pastries   92

Pancakes & Waffles   118

Flans & Savouries   128

Basic Recipes   148

Index   158

Conversion Charts   160

Don't think of all the things you can't have – think of all the things you can …

INTRODUCTION

If you are reading this book it probably means that something has happened to you, or to someone you know, and you have to live without flour as part of your diet. Perhaps just for a short time, or perhaps for years. While much of what you eat will be as before, with plenty of salads and fruit, you may begin to wonder what you can have to replace the usual baked items that now form a regular part of most people's diet.

As a nation we have come to enjoy having a slice of toast or a sandwich at some time during the day, with perhaps a biscuit or a slice of cake with coffee at the weekend. All these are foods that will now be forbidden – along with the pancakes, waffles, pastries, lasagnes and everything else that features flour in some form. I know exactly how difficult it is to totally exclude flour and starchy foods from the diet as I have lived this way for over ten years. But I no longer feel deprived or different for one single second, as I have all of the above, and more, and all flour-free and totally delicious.

These recipes are for anyone who needs to exclude all types of flour from their diet, or has to cook for someone who needs to, but longs for something as simple as a piece of quiche or a chocolate biscuit. In my case it was the sudden and dramatic appearance of a record-breaking-size rash that heralded my new life without flour, and for several years I managed on very simple and plain meals. Determined that there must be a way to enjoy baked staples again I began experimenting – my scientist grandfather had once told me that cooking was elementary laboratory work – and, many rather odd results later, I finally produced recipes for breads, cakes, biscuits, pastries and more that worked. They are made with natural ingredients and contain no gluten or yeast. And, just like normal cakes and biscuits, they'll make you fat if you eat too many of them!

While certainly not advocating a life of biscuits and puddings, it is wonderful to once again have the choice of eating something as simple as a chunk of bread, or a couple of waffles with maple syrup. Whatever your reasons for avoiding flour I hope there is something in this collection, even if you're new to home baking, to tempt you to try the recipes. After you've glanced through the pages, take five minutes to read through the notes section on pages 8–11. As many of the recipes use similar methods for melting chocolate, sifting and mixing, I have given more detail in the notes to save repeating it throughout. All the recipes are straightforward, use few ingredients, and look and taste as satisfying as the originals they replace. There are a few recipes, such as the pancakes and waffles and one or two savouries, which strictly speaking don't belong in a baking book, as they are not baked. However, as they use flour as a major ingredient, I felt they should be included.

Lastly, as these recipes contain nuts, it is important, as with all recipes, to check before serving that all the ingredients used are suitable for the intended recipient. Also, where a brand name has been mentioned it does not guarantee that that particular product is, or will remain, totally flour-free. Therefore, always check the labels of pre-prepared ingredients for any possible grain or flour inclusions before using.

We don't have to do it that way just because we always have …

NOTES

Anyone who has made whisked sponges will be familiar with the principles of preparing many of the recipes in this book – there is nothing difficult about any of them. It is worth reading through the recipe completely and getting all the ingredients and tins ready before starting, as some of the recipes have to be prepared for the oven quickly once the egg whites are whisked. Most of the recipes are quick to prepare and use relatively few ingredients. Yet they lose nothing in taste. Do take the time to read through these notes before starting as they explain why some usual ingredients are omitted and others used instead.

Starch as an added ingredient. Starch from grain is now so widely added to many of our everyday pre-prepared foods that it is becoming very difficult to avoid it unless you undertake most of your own food preparation. It really is a case of going back to basics. Some foods can contain starch or wheat products even though it is not always declared as such in the ingredients. I have been caught out with salad dressings, and glucose-syrup-coated dried fruit – the glucose syrup was made from wheat. Many of the supermarkets now list the allergens on the packaging of their own brands and this is a great help. Read every label, and if you're not sure, ask. There are very good allergy books available in bookshops that explain the various terms used for particular grains or starch in labelling. I used to refer constantly to such books until I got used to what they all were. I still check the labels every time I buy, as ingredients can change.

Oven temperatures and fan-assisted ovens. If you prefer to use a fan-assisted oven please refer to your oven manual for equivalent temperature settings, usually 10–20 ° C lower than regular oven settings, and allow roughly the same cooking times. The recipes were tested in both types of electric oven and both gave equally good results, with the regular oven providing a slightly darker finish. Keep in mind that ovens can vary a lot, and conversions of cooking temperatures are not exact. Having cooked in unreliable ovens at high altitude I am used to making small adjustments as necessary when trying a new recipe. You will know from your usual cooking whether you need to adjust the temperature settings and timings a little either way.

Spoon sizes. All measurements are level spoonfuls unless otherwise stated. Tablespoon (tblsp) is 15 ml. Dessert spoon (dstsp) is 10 ml. Teaspoon (tsp) is 5 ml.

All-purpose food wrap. Use a good quality food wrap when rolling out biscuits and pastry as it is easier to handle. Avoid the thin, stretchy, cling wraps suitable only for covering containers. Or use baking parchment or greaseproof paper instead, although it may be necessary to patch pastry after lifting it into the tin.

Baking tins. Good bakeware lasts years and more than repays the initial investment. I use both good quality non-stick bakeware and the anodised cake tins that are readily available. Loose based tins are useful for cakes; use the new deeper tins for layer cakes. Non-stick is best for breads, small cakes, biscuits and mince pies. Flans and quiches cook well in greased loose based ordinary flan tins. Grease the tins before using even if non-stick.

Greasing and lining tins. To grease tins for cakes use melted butter brushed on with a pastry brush to give an even layer. For the breads use olive oil to grease the tins. Use baking parchment to line tins, cutting the corners for square tins. You can buy circles of baking parchment for base lining, and narrow rolls for lining the sides of tins. The secret for lining tins is to grease the tin before putting the lining paper in so it sticks in place, then lightly grease the paper.

Filling tins. It is important to remember that the mixture comes out of the oven just about the same size and shape as it went in. Some of the cakes will rise a little when they start cooking but will sink back almost to the original size as they bake. When filling tins – in particular shaped tins for sponge flans or ring moulds – make sure the mixture has no air pockets in the sides or edges. Otherwise it will have holes and dents in the edge!

Eggs. The egg size is very important. Always use very fresh medium sized eggs weighing between 50–55 g each. As so many eggs are used I always use organic eggs. Don't be tempted to use larger eggs in the hope of getting a more risen bread or cake – the chances are that you will end up with most of it on the oven floor and a sorry offering left in the baking pan! If the eggs used are much larger or smaller adjust the number used. If necessary weigh them and try a few different ones to get the right weight, or use part of an egg if necessary. Use eggs at room temperature.

Whisking egg whites. Always make sure the bowl is completely grease free. Use an electric mixer if possible. Whisk the whites until very stiff indeed, much more than you may be used to. Don't worry, you won't over-beat them. Use the whites as soon as they are ready.

Adding yolks. It is best to use a wire whisk to do this. You can be fairly brisk in the mixing, continuing until the mix is a nice even colour.

Folding in. Really the same as making a sponge cake. Use a nice big metal spoon – the bigger the better – and cut and fold the dry ingredients into the egg. It gets easier with practice. Avoid over mixing as air will be lost.

Ground almonds. These are widely available. Some are more finely ground than others, so use the finest available. Where a recipe calls for sifting the ground almonds and icing sugar together do take the time to do it. It only takes a couple of minutes, and helps to incorporate air into the mixture and combines the ingredients well. Discard any large pieces of nut left in the sieve.

Icing sugar. Read the ingredients label carefully. Some have added ingredients to make different types of icing. Use a plain icing sugar.

Cake decorations. It is difficult to find coloured cake decorations that don't contain any grain or flour in some form. I tend to use either grated chocolate or bought sprinkles that have no starch listed on the ingredients label. Be careful to check every ingredient if you are very sensitive, or are cooking for someone who is.

Baking powder. I have not found a commercial baking powder that doesn't contain starch in some form, although there are gluten-free ones available. For this reason I make up a very basic baking powder for the very few recipes that use it. Recipe as follows: Mix 1 tblsp bicarbonate of soda with 3 tblsp cream of tartar. Sift together 4 times and store in a tightly lidded jar. Use as directed in recipes.

Chocolate. Always read the label and check that it doesn't contain any wheat, grain, flour or malt inclusions if you are sensitive to any of these. I have to be cautious with chocolate as it can give me a headache but I do love the taste.

Melting chocolate. Break the chocolate into pieces and put them in a bowl over a pan of barely simmering water. Do not let the water boil or touch the bottom of the bowl. As soon as the chocolate is melted stir until smooth, allow to cool a little and use as required. For small amounts of chocolate put the pieces in a cup and stand the cup in a bowl of very hot water. It only takes a minute or two to melt a few pieces for decoration this way.

Glucose syrup. Now widely used in food manufacturing. As glucose syrup can be made from wheat, or other grain, I avoid it.

Glacé cherries, candied peel, dried cherries, blueberries and cranberries. I have not found any glacé cherries or candied peel that don't have glucose syrup in them – see above. Instead I substitute dried cherries, cranberries or blueberries for glacé cherries.

Cheese. None of these recipes use blue cheese, which could contain minute amounts of gluten in the mould. Be sure to read the label of soft cheeses as sometimes these can contain starch. Some pre-grated cheeses can also contain potato or other starch to separate the strands. I use mostly goat-milk or sheep-milk cheeses as I find them more digestible, but use whichever type you prefer.

Apples. None of the recipes use cooking apples, which are too starchy and indigestible for me. I always use a floury eating apple such as Golden Delicious instead, but if it's not a problem to you, use which you prefer and adjust the sugar to taste.

Marzipan. Many brands contain glucose syrup so I make my own – this is very easy to do – from the included recipe.

Black pepper and spices. None of these recipes use pepper or spices as they don't agree with me due to their starch content. By all means include them if you can eat them.

Butter. When buying butter for using in these recipes choose one that is very firm when chilled – the harder the better. This makes the biscuits and pastries crisper. Bring to room temperature before using.

Ghee. One or two of the recipes use ghee, made from butter, which should be readily available in most supermarkets.

Storing and freezing the breads. While the breads are best eaten fresh they will keep for a couple of days if stored in a polythene bag in the fridge. They will also freeze successfully for up to a month if they are open frozen and then packed in a rigid airtight container. Allow to thaw at room temperature before using.

USEFUL EQUIPMENT

These recipes are easy to make using a simple range of basic cooking equipment. Most kitchens have many of the following items, but if not it is probably worth purchasing any missing pieces. Good quality kitchen equipment is easy and enjoyable to use – and will help give you confidence to try some of the more detailed recipes if you are a novice cook. After acquiring the basics, any kitchen gadgets that will enhance your cooking enjoyment can be added.

Table-top mixer or hand-held mixer. Either of these will do the job. I have a table-top mixer because it means I can get on with another part of the recipe while it mixes, beats and whisks. But it is a large purchase and a hand-held mixer will do the job as well. Some electric hand mixers are available with an optional stand.

Weighing scales. Use a good set of scales with no more than five-gram increments. Balance scales are easy to use, can weigh small amounts accurately, and are easy to change from imperial to metric – simply change the weights.

Mixing bowls. A large one for whisking egg whites and several smaller ones.

Baking tins. These are usually added to over the years. Whenever you purchase new ones choose good quality higher-sided tins. Good baking tins are worth any extra outlay and last longer.

Pastry brush. For greasing baking tins.

Non-stick baking parchment – rolls and pre-cut discs.

Metal sieve. For sifting dry ingredients.

Wire whisk. For mixing in the egg yolks.

Large metal spoon. For folding in dry ingredients.

Plastic or rubber spatula. For scraping the last of the mixture into baking tins.

Fish slice. For removing biscuits from baking trays.

Cooling racks.

Chopping board.

Wooden spoons and spatulas. For stirring sauces and rolling brandy snaps.

Sharp knives that really are sharp.

Rolling pin.

Biscuit cutters.

Grater.

Lemon zester – for paring rind.

Lemon juicer.

Measuring spoons.

Scissors.

Small freezer bags or icing set.

Food piping bag and large plain nozzle.

Waffle iron.

Double boiler. Useful but not essential.

BREADS

Of all the things you miss on a flour-free diet this has to one of the biggest. What is a bowl of soup without a chunk of buttered bread on the side? Or Sunday morning without toast and thick orange marmalade? Or sweet rolls if you prefer. I confess it was the desire for bread that forced me to start experimenting. Quite simply I longed for a ham-and-mustard sandwich to take on picnics to the beach – the simplest of foods but so easily taken for granted. After the Basic Bread recipe the more sophisticated breads followed, but the basic one is the most useful. It makes sandwiches, toast, soldiers for dipping in boiled eggs, and is the base for toasted cheese or other snacks. The sweeter breads have an altogether more continental flavour and the Christmas Breads are a delicious alternative to the well-known Stollen Bread, while the Sultana and Poppy Seed Bread can be eaten as is or toasted. It also makes a pretty good biscotti to have with coffee, but don't be tempted to dunk it – it disappears! One of the greatest things about these breads is the ease and speed with which they can be prepared and cooked – the Basic Bread takes approximately half an hour from start to finish – and all are easy to make as there's no waiting for yeast to rise and no kneading. You'll find a bread for most purposes in this chapter and even a very good Pecan Danish to have with coffee.

We could have a sandwich for lunch if we could eat bread ...

This is a very good basic bread. It is very quick and easy to make, toasts well, and is a good base for cheese on toast or other toasted snacks. Get everything ready before you start – it needs to be baked as soon as it is mixed.

BASIC BREAD

4 eggs – separated

Pinch of salt – optional

115 g ground almonds

Non-stick baking tin 20 x 24 cm, oiled

Oven temperature 180°C/350°F/Gas 4

Makes one flat bread 20 x 24 cm.

Put the egg yolks in a cup, with salt if using, and beat well with a fork. Whisk the egg whites with an electric beater until very stiff. Pour the yolks over the top and mix thoroughly using a wire whisk.

Sprinkle the ground almonds over the top and fold in lightly using a large metal spoon. Using a spatula transfer the mixture to the prepared tin and smooth the top.

Bake in a pre-heated oven for about 18–20 minutes until nicely browned and firm. Cool for a few minutes in the tin and then turn out. Cut into 6 even sized squares.

TO TOAST: *(See photograph on page 14.)* Cut each piece through the middle to make 2 even-sized slices. Toast under a pre-heated grill, watching carefully as the outsides toast quickly. Serve in a toast rack just as you would toast. Perfect with butter and marmalade.

VARIATION: Sprinkle the top with sesame seeds or poppy seeds before baking as above. This is delicious as toast or for making sandwiches.

SUN-DRIED TOMATO & ROSEMARY BREAD

Makes one flat bread 20 x 24 cm.

Put the egg yolks in a cup and beat well with a fork.

Whisk the egg whites with an electric beater until very stiff. Pour the yolks over the top and mix thoroughly using a wire whisk.

Sprinkle the ground almonds over the top and fold in lightly using a large metal spoon. Transfer the mixture to the prepared tin and smooth the top.

Drain the sun-dried tomatoes and snip each into several pieces. Arrange on top of the mixture. Break off small sprigs of rosemary and place between the tomatoes.

Bake in a pre-heated oven for about 18–20 minutes until nicely browned and firm. Cool for a few minutes in the tin and then turn out. Cut into 6 even-sized pieces.

Delicious served with soup, or with cheese and salad as a light meal.

4 eggs – separated

115 g ground almonds

6 halves of sun-dried tomato in oil

2 or 3 sprigs of fresh rosemary

Non-stick baking tin 20 x 24 cm, oiled

Oven temperature 180°C/350°F/Gas 4

HERB BREAD

4 eggs – separated

120 g ground almonds

1 tsp dried mixed herbs

¼ tsp salt – optional

Sprigs of fresh rosemary

Non-stick baking tin
24 x 20 cm, oiled

Oven temperature
180°C/350° F/Gas 4

Makes one 24 x 20 cm flat bread.

Put the egg yolks in a cup and beat well with a fork.

Mix the ground almonds with the herbs and salt if using.

Whisk the egg whites until very stiff. Pour the yolks over the top and mix thoroughly using a wire whisk.

Sprinkle the almond mix over the top and fold in using a large metal spoon. Turn into the prepared tin and arrange the rosemary sprigs over the top.

Bake in a pre-heated oven for about 20 minutes until lightly browned and firm to the touch. Leave in the tin for a few minutes, then turn onto a cooling rack to cool.

Delicious with soup.

CHEESE & ONION BREAD

Makes one 24 x 20 cm flat bread.

Slice the onion wafer thin. Put into a bowl, add the oil and mix well.

Put the egg yolks in a cup and mix well with a fork.

Mix the ground almonds with the cheese.

Whisk the egg whites until very stiff. Pour the yolks over the whites and mix thoroughly using a wire whisk. Sprinkle the almond mix over the top and fold in carefully using a large metal spoon. Using a spatula turn the mixture into the prepared tin. Scatter the onion over the top.

Bake in a pre-heated oven for about 20 minutes until the onions are browned and the bread is firm. Leave in the tin for a few minutes, then turn out onto a rack to cool.

Delicious served with a mixed green salad for a light lunch.

1 small onion

1 tblsp olive oil

4 eggs – separated

120 g ground almonds

50 g pecorino cheese – very finely grated

Non-stick baking tin 24 x 20 cm, oiled

Oven temperature 180°C/350°F/Gas 4

BLACK OLIVE & FETA CHEESE BREAD

4 eggs – separated

100 g feta cheese

115 g ground almonds

18 black olives – stoned

Non-stick baking tin
20 x 24 cm, oiled

Oven temperature
180°C/350°F/Gas 4

Makes one flat bread 20 x 24 cm.

Put the egg yolks in a cup and mix well with a fork.

Cut the feta cheese into small pieces (less than 1 cm square).

Whisk the egg whites until very stiff. Pour the yolks over the top and mix thoroughly using a wire whisk.

Sprinkle the almonds over the top and fold in using a very large metal spoon. Sprinkle the cheese on the top and stir just enough to mix through. Pour into the prepared tin and smooth the top.

Arrange the olives on top. Bake in a pre-heated oven for about 20 minutes until firm to the touch. Leave in the tin until fairly cool before turning out.

CHEESE & PINE NUT ROLLS

90 g ground almonds

50 g cheddar-type cheese – finely grated

3 eggs – separated

1 tblsp pine nuts

9 cm Yorkshire pudding tins, greased

Oven temperature 180°C/350°F/Gas 4

Makes 4.

Mix the ground almonds with the cheese.

Beat the egg yolks well with a fork.

Whisk the egg whites until very stiff. Pour the yolks over and mix thoroughly using a wire whisk. Sprinkle the almond mixture over the top and fold in carefully using a large metal spoon.

Divide between the prepared tins, slightly doming the tops. Sprinkle the pine nuts over the top.

Bake in a pre-heated oven for 20 minutes until browned and firm. Turn out onto a cooling rack until cold.

Split and fill for picnics, packed lunches or snacks. These are a nice alternative to cheese scones.

An excellent bun for using as a burger bun, or as a filled roll.

SESAME BAPS

5 eggs – separated

140 g ground almonds

¼ tsp salt

Sesame seeds

9 cm Yorkshire pudding tins, greased

Oven temperature
180°C/350°F/Gas 4

Makes 8.

Put the egg yolks in a cup and beat well with a fork.

Sift the ground almonds with the salt.

Whisk the egg whites until very stiff. Pour the yolks over the top and mix well together using a wire whisk.

Sprinkle the almonds over the top and fold together using a very large metal spoon.

Spoon into the prepared tins and dome the tops. Sprinkle sesame seeds on top.

Bake in a pre-heated oven for 18–20 minutes until lightly browned and firm to the touch. Cool for a few minutes in the tins then lift out onto cooling racks.

TO USE AS BURGER BUNS: Slice the buns through the middle and toast if required. Season minced beef or lamb with salt and dried herbs. Shape into patties and fry or grill until cooked through. Serve in the buns with salad leaves, starch-free ketchup or mustard. A slice of cheese may be placed on top of the burger. Grill until melted and then replace the tops.

VARIATION: Poppy seed buns. Replace the sesame seeds with poppy seeds and make as above.

TOASTED TEA CAKES

Makes 4.

Sift the ground almonds with the icing sugar twice. Stir in the currants and the orange or lemon rind.

Beat the egg yolks well with a fork.

Whisk the egg whites until very stiff. Pour the yolks over and mix in thoroughly using a wire whisk. Sprinkle the almond mix over the top and fold in using a large metal spoon. Divide between the prepared tins and smooth the tops to make a nice dome.

Bake in a pre-heated oven for about 20 minutes until browned and firm.

Cool on a rack.

Split through the middle, toast on both sides and serve warm with butter.

90 g ground almonds

10 g icing sugar

100 g currants

Grated rind of ½ lemon or orange

3 eggs – separated

9 cm Yorkshire pudding tins, well greased

Oven temperature 170°C/325°F/Gas 3

CHRISTMAS BREADS

100 g icing sugar

180 g ground almonds

30 g flaked almonds

50 g dried cranberries

50 g sultanas

50 g chopped candied peel
(see recipe on page 156)

Grated rind of 1 orange

4 eggs – separated

½ tsp vanilla essence

½ tsp lemon essence

6 non-stick mini kougelhopf tins (approximately 250 ml in size), well greased with melted butter

Oven temperature 170°C/325°F/Gas 3

These are easy to make and perfect for breakfast in bed on Christmas morning while unwrapping Santa's presents. Makes 6.

Sift icing sugar and ground almonds together. Dust the greased moulds with a teaspoon of the mix, knocking the excess back into the bowl.

Add the flaked almonds, cranberries, sultanas, peel and grated rind to the icing sugar mixture and stir well. Mix the egg yolks with the essences.

Whisk the egg whites until very stiff. Pour the yolks over the top and mix together using a wire whisk. Sprinkle the almond mix on top and stir together using a large metal spoon.

Spoon the mix into the prepared moulds and level the tops. Bake in a pre-heated oven for about 25 minutes until brown and firm to the touch. Cool in the tins for 10 minutes, then turn out onto a cooling rack until cold.

Dust with icing sugar to serve. Eat as they are or serve with lemon or orange curd, or jam.

DATE & WALNUT SWIRL

Makes one 16 cm square flat bread.

Mix **half** the walnuts with the sugar and set aside.

Snip the dates into pieces.

Mix ground almonds, dates and remaining walnuts together. Stir well.

Beat egg yolks with a fork until well mixed.

Whisk egg whites until very stiff. Pour the yolks over the top and mix thoroughly using a wire whisk. Sprinkle the almond mix over the top and fold in using a large metal spoon. Using a spatula turn the mixture into the prepared tin.

Sprinkle the sugar and walnut mixture over the top. Lightly pull a chopstick or spoon handle through the mixture to roughen the top and slightly pull the topping into the mix.

Bake in a pre-heated oven for 25–30 minutes until firm when pressed in the centre. Cool for a few minutes in the tin, then turn out onto a rack and leave until cold before cutting.

Serve in slices with a little butter or jam.

50 g walnut halves – chopped

2 tblsp light brown muscovado sugar

100 g Medjool or other soft stoned dates

100 g ground almonds

3 eggs – separated

Non-stick cake tin 16 cm square, well greased

Oven temperature 170°C/325°F/Gas 3

SULTANA & POPPY SEED BREAD

100 g ground almonds

50 g sultanas

1 tblsp muscovado sugar

2 tsp poppy seeds

3 eggs – separated

1 tsp muscovado sugar mixed with ½ tsp poppy seeds to finish

Non-stick cake tin 16 cm square, well greased

Oven temperature 170°C/325°F/Gas 3

Makes one 16 cm square flat bread.

Mix the ground almonds, sultanas, sugar and poppy seeds together.

Beat the egg yolks with a fork.

Whisk the egg whites until very stiff. Pour the yolks over and mix thoroughly using a wire whisk. Sprinkle the almond mix over the top and fold together using a large metal spoon. Spoon into the prepared tin and level the top. Sprinkle the sugar and poppy seed mix evenly over the top.

Bake in a pre-heated oven for 20–25 minutes until firm. Cool in the tin for 10 minutes, then turn onto a rack and leave until cold before slicing.

Serve on its own or with a little butter or jam.

VARIATION: Biscotti. Slice the cooled bread into 1½ cm slices. Stand upright on a baking tray and bake at 100°C/200°F/Gas ¼ for about 40 minutes until crisp. These are more fragile than regular biscotti, but still very good. Don't try dunking them however, as they disappear.

PECAN DANISH

Makes one 20 cm round sweet bread.

Mix the egg yolks with the vanilla essence.

Sift the ground almonds with the 20 g of icing sugar.

Mix the brown sugar with the apricot jam, blending to a smooth paste.

Whisk the egg whites until very stiff. Pour the yolks over and mix thoroughly using a wire whisk. Sprinkle the almond mix on top and mix together carefully using a large metal spoon. Take a teaspoonful of the mix and stir into the apricot and sugar mixture. Spoon the rest into the prepared tin.

Using a teaspoon, dot spoonfuls of the apricot mix over the top of the bread, then use a chopstick or spoon handle to slightly pull the mixture through the bread. Do not try to mix it in – do less rather than more.

Bake in a pre-heated oven for about 20–25 minutes until firm and browned on top. Cool for a few minutes, then turn out onto a cooling rack until cold.

Mix the icing sugar with just enough water to make a slightly runny icing. Place the pecans over the top of the bread and drizzle the icing over the top. Leave to set and serve cut in wedges.

3 eggs – separated

1 tsp vanilla essence

100 g ground almonds

20 g icing sugar

3 tblsp light brown muscovado sugar

2 tblsp apricot jam

50 g icing sugar

10–12 pecan halves

20 cm round loose-based sandwich tin, well greased, base-lined and greased again

Oven temperature 180°C/350°F/Gas 4

16–20 whole almonds

100 g icing sugar

170 g ground almonds

140 g raisins

4 eggs – separated

½ tsp vanilla essence

*Non-stick kougelhopf mould,
16 cm diameter, well
greased with melted butter*

*Oven temperature
170°C/325°F/Gas 3*

KOUGELHOPF

*A cross between a bread and a cake, this is absolutely delicious and
very easy to make. Serve on its own with a glass of Alsace wine, or eat
with butter, jam or fruit for breakfast or tea. Makes one bread.*

Place the whole almonds in a design in the bottom of the mould.

Mix the icing sugar and ground almonds together and sift once. Stir in
the raisins.

Beat yolks with a fork and add the essence.

Whisk whites until very stiff. Pour the yolks over the whites and mix thoroughly
using a wire whisk. Sprinkle the almond mixture over the top and fold in
carefully using a large metal spoon.

Spoon into the prepared mould, filling to within ½–1 cm of the top and
bake in a pre-heated oven for 35–45 minutes until firm and browned.

Cool in the tin for a few minutes then turn out onto a cooling rack and
cool completely before cutting. May be dusted with icing sugar to serve.

VARIATION: Currant & Hazelnut Kougelhopf.

(see photograph on page 6).

Omit the whole almonds. Sprinkle 2 tblsp chopped toasted hazelnuts around the greased tin, tapping the tin to distribute the nuts evenly.

Omit the raisins and vanilla essence. Use 140 g currants and 1 tsp natural lemon extract. Make as above.

When cool, ice the top with a little glacé icing made with 6 tblsp icing sugar, allowing the icing to run over the sides. Sprinkle 1 tblsp roasted chopped hazelnuts onto the icing before it sets.

....

SWEET ROLLS

Makes 8–12 depending on tin size.

Sift the ground almonds and the icing sugar together twice.

Beat the egg yolks well with a fork.

Whisk the egg whites until very stiff. Pour the yolks over and mix together thoroughly with a wire whisk. Sprinkle the almonds over the top and fold in carefully, using a large metal spoon.

Spoon the mixture into the tins, filling them well.

Bake in a pre-heated oven for 18–20 minutes, depending on size, until firm to the touch and lightly browned.

Tip out onto a rack and leave until cold.

150 g ground almonds

25 g icing sugar

5 eggs – separated

Brioche or muffin tins, well greased

Oven temperature 170°C/325°F/Gas 3

CAKES

Once I discovered a way to make light and delicious totally flour-free cakes, I was hooked! I really missed coffee and walnut cake, and lemon cake. Now I have something from this section whenever I can think of an excuse, and I thoroughly enjoy every previously forbidden morsel. As I have to forego cakes when out, these delicious treats are my one indulgence. If you have to go without regular cake you won't need to feel deprived with something from this chapter on the menu. There are cakes for every occasion, from a rich fruit cake for Christmas or Easter and little cup cakes and iced teatime treats, to sponge fingers and luxurious Sachertorte. Some, like the iced French Fancies, take longer to make while others, such as the Layered Lemon Squares, are fairly quick but equally delicious. If you haven't been able to eat cake for days, weeks, months or years you're sure to be tempted by the recipes in this chapter.

It's rather hard to feel deprived after eating chocolate layer cake ...

40 g cocoa powder

200 g icing sugar

140 g ground almonds

6 eggs – separated

½ tsp vanilla essence

ICING

2 tblsp cocoa powder

2 tblsp boiling water

125 g soft unsalted butter

½ tsp vanilla essence

250 g sifted icing sugar

25 g dark chocolate, melted
– optional (see notes)

*Two 20 cm loose-based
cake tins, greased, base-
lined and greased again*

*Oven temperature
170°C/325°F/Gas 3*

CHOCOLATE LAYER CAKE

Makes one 20 cm layer cake. (Also see photograph on page 30.)

Sift cocoa, icing sugar and ground almonds together twice. Beat the egg yolks and the vanilla essence together.

Whisk the egg whites until very stiff. Pour the yolks over the top and mix thoroughly using a wire whisk. Sprinkle the almond mix on top and fold in lightly using a large metal spoon. Spoon the mixture into the prepared tins and level the tops.

Bake in a pre-heated oven for 25–30 minutes until the cakes are firm to the touch and the sides have shrunk slightly away from the tin. Cool for 10 minutes in the tins, then turn out onto cooling racks until cold.

TO MAKE THE ICING: Dissolve the cocoa in the boiling water and mix to a smooth paste. Beat the butter and cocoa mix together until creamy. Beat in the vanilla essence. Add the icing sugar and beat until blended and smooth. Stir in the melted chocolate if using. Use half to sandwich the cake together and spread the remainder on top.

COCONUT MADELEINES

Makes 6–7 individual cakes.

Sift the icing sugar and ground almonds together twice. Mix the egg yolks with the essence. Whisk the egg whites until very stiff.

Pour the yolks over the whites and mix together thoroughly using a wire whisk. Sprinkle the almond mix on top and use a large metal spoon to mix together. Spoon into the moulds, filling almost to the top. Set the moulds on a baking tray and bake in a pre-heated oven for about 18–20 minutes until firm and nicely browned. The mix may rise up and sink back a little during baking but it won't matter.

Remove from the oven and cool a little in the tins, then turn onto a cooling rack and leave until cold. Trim the bases to neaten and so the cakes stand straight.

Sieve the jam and brush over the top and sides of the cakes, then roll in the coconut. Leave to set. These are traditionally decorated with a glacé cherry, but see notes before using.

| 50 g icing sugar |
| 75 g ground almonds |
| 2 eggs – separated |
| ¼ tsp vanilla essence |
| 3–4 tblsp sugar-free red jam |
| desiccated coconut |

Small dariole moulds, very well greased

Oven temperature 180°C/350°F/Gas 4

FRENCH MADELEINES

60 g ground almonds

2 eggs

60 g caster sugar

Finely grated rind of 1 small lemon

15 g unsalted butter – melted and cooled

Icing sugar to finish

A madeleine tray (shell shapes), very well greased

Oven temperature 200°C/400°F/Gas 6

These little cakes make a nice accompaniment to fruit for dessert. Makes 12.

Sift the ground almonds twice.

Whisk the eggs and sugar to the ribbon stage – when the whisk is lifted out it leaves a ribbon of mix that keeps its shape for about 10 seconds. Stir in the lemon rind.

Pour the melted butter into a small jug, leaving the sediment behind as much as possible. Take two tablespoons of the egg mix and add to the butter, mixing thoroughly.

Sprinkle ¾ of the ground almonds over the egg mix and fold in using a large metal spoon. Fold in the remaining ground almonds along with the butter mix, using gentle cutting and folding to distribute the butter evenly. Chill the mixture in the bowl for 20 minutes to allow the butter to firm.

Spoon into the prepared tin, filling each shell almost to the top. Bake in a pre-heated oven for about 10 minutes until brown and firm to the touch.

Leave in the tin for a few minutes and then transfer to a rack to cool, shell side uppermost. Serve plain or dusted with icing sugar.

COFFEE & WALNUT LAYER CAKE

Makes one 20 cm layer cake.

Dissolve the coffee granules in the boiling water and then whisk in the egg yolks and vanilla essence. Sift the ground almonds and the icing sugar together twice.

Whisk the egg whites until very stiff. Pour the yolk mix over the top and fold in using a wire whisk. Sprinkle the almond mix on top and fold in lightly using a metal spoon. Divide between the prepared tins and bake in a pre-heated oven for about 30 minutes until evenly cooked and firm to the touch. Leave in the tins to cool, then turn onto racks and leave until cold.

If the cakes have sunk a little in the centre and you would like a more traditional appearance, trim the risen edges level using a sharp bread knife.

TO MAKE THE ICING: Beat the icing sugar and butter together until pale and fluffy. Beat in the coffee mixture. Use half the mix to sandwich the cake layers together. Spread the remaining mixture on top, using a knife to swirl the icing. Arrange the walnut halves around the edge.

1 ½ tblsp coffee granules

1 dstsp boiling water

6 eggs – separated

½ tsp vanilla essence

180 g ground almonds

180 g icing sugar

ICING
This quantity gives a generous topping and filling

280 g sifted icing sugar

140 g soft unsalted butter

1 ½ tblsp coffee granules dissolved in 1 tblsp hot water

Walnut halves to finish

Two 20 cm round loose-based sandwich-cake tins, greased, base-lined and greased again

Oven temperature 170°C/325°F/Gas 3

FRUIT CAKE

250 g currants

150 g sultanas

100 g raisins

100 g dried cranberries

Grated rind of 1 orange and
1 lemon

4 tblsp orange juice

4 tblsp brandy

200 g ground almonds

160 g soft brown sugar

4 eggs – separated

1 tsp almond essence

Whole almonds to decorate

*20 cm loose-based tin, base
and sides greased and lined
with a double thickness of
baking parchment and
greased again*

*Oven temperature
150°C/300°F/Gas 2*

Makes one 20 cm round cake.

Put the currants, sultanas, raisins, cranberries and grated rind in a large bowl. Pour over the orange juice and brandy and stir well. Leave to soak for several hours or overnight.

Sift the ground almonds and sugar together twice. Beat the egg yolks and essence with a fork.

Whisk the egg whites until very stiff. Pour the yolks over and mix thoroughly using a wire whisk. Add the soaked fruits to the eggs and stir together. Sprinkle the almond and sugar mixture over the top and use a large metal spoon to cut and fold into the mixture. Spoon into the prepared tin and level the top. Decorate with whole almonds.

Fold two sheets of newspaper into a band and tie around the tin to stop the cake browning too much on the outside. Stand the tin on a few sheets of folded newspaper in a pre-heated oven and bake for 3–3½ hours until firm to the touch and a skewer inserted in the centre comes out clean. If the top starts to brown too much put a piece of baking paper over the top.

Leave to cool in the tin for 1 hour and then turn out onto a rack. Leave until cold before cutting.

NOTE: This recipe doesn't contain any spices. If you can tolerate spices then sift 1 tsp ground mixed spice and 1 tsp ground cinnamon with the ground almonds and omit the almond essence.

130 g icing sugar

100 g ground almonds

20 g cocoa

4 eggs – separated

½ tsp coffee granules

½ tsp boiling water

FILLING

100 g soft unsalted butter

200 g sifted icing sugar

1 tblsp hot water

Few drops vanilla essence

32 x 22 cm swiss-roll tin, greased, lined with baking parchment, and greased again

Oven temperature 170°C/325°F/Gas 3

CHOCOLATE SWISS ROLL

Makes one cake.

Sift the icing sugar, ground almonds and cocoa together, making sure they are well mixed. Beat the egg yolks with a fork. Dissolve the coffee in the boiling water and then beat into the yolks.

Whisk the egg whites until very stiff. Pour the yolks over the top and mix in thoroughly using a wire whisk. Sprinkle the almond mix on top and fold in lightly using a large metal spoon. Put into the prepared tin and level the top. Bake in a pre-heated oven for 20–25 minutes until firm to the touch. Leave in the tin until only just cool.

TO MAKE THE FILLING: Beat the butter until soft then beat in the icing sugar and the hot water and continue beating until light and fluffy. Beat in the essence.

Slide the cake out onto the worktop, keeping the lining paper in place underneath. Peel back the edges of the paper. Use a very sharp knife to trim ½ cm from the cake edges and then spread with the filling. Using the lining paper, lift the short edge of the cake and start to roll it, pulling the cake into a roll and easing away the paper as it turns. Turn onto a plate and dust with icing sugar. Put in a cool place to set the filling.

NOTE: The cake is rolled upside down to help prevent cracking. Filling and rolling as soon as the cake is just cooled also helps, as the cake is more pliable than when completely cold.

ICED VANILLA CUP CAKES

Makes 12–15.

Cream the butter and sugar until very pale and fluffy. Mix the essence with the beaten egg. Add the egg and the almonds to the butter mix and beat all together.

Spoon into the paper cases and bake in a pre-heated oven for 18–20 minutes until risen and browned. Transfer to a cooling rack until cold.

ICING: Mix the icing sugar with just enough orange juice to make a coating consistency. Spread a little in the centre of each cake and decorate with chocolate sprinkles.

VARIATION: Almond cup cakes. Replace the vanilla essence with almond essence and bake as above. Omit the icing. Melt 50 g milk chocolate and spread a little in the centre of each cake. Top with a plain or toasted almond.

100 g soft unsalted butter

100 g sifted icing sugar

1 tsp vanilla essence

2 eggs beaten

125 g ground almonds – sifted

ICING

180 g sifted icing sugar

3 tblsp strained orange juice

Chocolate sprinkles (see notes)

Bun tray lined with cup-cake cases

Oven temperature 180°C/350°F/Gas 4

CHOCOLATE SPONGE FINGERS

50 g ground almonds

10 g cocoa powder

3 egg whites

80 g sifted icing sugar

1 tsp cocoa powder and
1 tsp icing sugar mixed
together

40 g white or milk chocolate
(see notes)

*Baking trays lined with
baking parchment*

*Oven temperature
170°C/325°F/Gas 3*

Makes about 20.

Sift the ground almonds and cocoa together. Whisk egg whites until stiff. Whisk in the icing sugar a spoonful at a time, then continue whisking until it resembles meringue. Sprinkle the almond mixture over the top and fold in using a large metal spoon.

Spoon into a food piping bag fitted with a plain 1.3 cm nozzle. Pipe fingers 1.5 cm wide and 9 cm long onto the prepared baking trays. Lightly sift a little cocoa and icing-sugar mix over the tops and leave to stand for one minute. Bake in a pre-heated oven for 15–20 minutes until firm on the outside but still soft in the middle. Transfer on the baking parchment to a cooling rack and leave until cold. Carefully peel off the parchment.

TO FINISH: Melt the chocolate. Spoon into a small freezer bag, snip off the corner and drizzle the chocolate over the tops of the fingers. Leave to set. Store in an airtight container.

VARIATION: Leave them plain, or sandwich them together with a little butter cream instead of decorating with chocolate.

COCONUT PICNIC SLICE

Makes 12 slices.

Mix the ground almonds, icing sugar, coconut, chocolate chips and cranberries together. Mix the egg yolks with the vanilla essence.

Whisk the egg whites until very stiff. Pour the yolks over and mix thoroughly using a wire whisk. Sprinkle the almond mix over the top and fold together using a large metal spoon. Turn into the prepared tin and smooth the top.

Bake in a pre-heated oven for about 20–25 minutes until firm to the touch and the sides have shrunk a little from the tin. Cool in the tin before turning out.

FOR THE TOPPING: Mix the icing sugar with just enough water to make a spreadable icing. Add a few drops of colouring if using. Spread on top of the picnic slice and sprinkle with the coconut. Leave to set before cutting into bars or squares.

VARIATION: Replace the cranberries with sultanas or raisins.

70 g ground almonds

50 g icing sugar

70 g desiccated coconut

50 g chocolate chips
(see notes)

40 g dried cranberries

4 eggs – separated

½ tsp vanilla essence

TOPPING

100 g icing sugar

Few drops pink natural food colouring – optional

Shredded or desiccated coconut to finish

24 x 20 cm non-stick cake tin, oiled

Oven temperature 180°C/350°F/Gas 4

FRENCH FANCIES

120 g icing sugar

120 g ground almonds

4 eggs – separated

FILLING AND ICING

5 tblsp apricot jam –
warmed

300 g marzipan
(see page 55)

230 g sifted icing sugar +
4 tblsp extra to finish

Pink and yellow natural food
colours

Good pinch cocoa powder

*Swiss-roll tin 30 x 20 cm,
greased, based-lined and
greased again*

*Oven temperature
170°C/325°F/Gas 3*

Makes 12.

Sift the icing sugar and almonds together twice. Beat the egg yolks with a fork. Whisk the whites until very stiff. Pour the yolks over the whites and mix in using a wire whisk.

Sprinkle the almond mix over the top and fold in using a large metal spoon. Spoon into the prepared tin and smooth the top. Bake in a pre-heated oven for about 25 minutes until evenly browned and firm. Cool in the tin.

Turn out and trim the edges to neaten. If necessary, trim the top level using a very sharp knife. Cut in half. Spread one half with 2 tblsp jam. Turn the second piece over, using the base as the top, and place on top. Cut into 12 squares.

MARZIPAN LAYER: Divide the marzipan into 12 and roll into balls. Sprinkle the worktop with a little icing sugar and roll out each ball until it is just large enough to cover the top and sides of a cake. Brush the marzipan with a little jam. Place on top of a cake and smooth the sides down, pinching the corners and trimming the excess. Form the trimmings into a roll and stick on top. Repeat with the others.

ICING: Mix the 230 g of icing sugar with just enough water to make a coating consistency. Divide in two and colour one half pale pink and the other half pale yellow. Spoon some icing on top of a cake and smooth over the sides with a knife. Do 6 of each colour. Place on a rack over a baking tray to catch the drips and leave until dry.

TO FINISH: Mix the 4 tblsp icing sugar with just enough water to make a piping icing. Divide in two. Leave one half white and colour the other half with a little cocoa powder. Spoon each into the corner of a small freezer bag, snip off the corner and drizzle the icing over the cakes. Leave to dry, then place in paper cases to serve.

40 g cocoa powder

200 g icing sugar

140 g ground almonds

6 eggs – separated

½ tsp vanilla essence

RASPBERRY BUTTER
CREAM

3 egg yolks

75 g granulated sugar

65 ml water

180 g soft unsalted butter

200 g raspberries – sieved

30–60 g sifted icing sugar

NOTE: Have all the filling ingredients at warm room temperature or the mixture may curdle. Keep the cake chilled once assembled.

CHOCOLATE LEAVES

18–20 unblemished rose leaves – washed and dried

50 g dark chocolate – melted (see notes)

Two 20 cm loose-based cake tins, greased, base-lined and greased again

Oven temperature 170°C/325°F/Gas 3

CHOCOLATE & RASPBERRY BUTTER CREAM CAKE

This is delicious – serve as a dessert for lunch or dinner. Makes one 20 cm layer cake.

Sift cocoa, icing sugar and ground almonds together twice. Beat egg yolks and vanilla essence with a fork.

Whisk the egg whites until very stiff. Pour the yolks over the top and mix thoroughly using a wire whisk. Sprinkle the almond mix on top and fold in using a large metal spoon. Spoon into the prepared tins and level tops.

Bake in a pre-heated oven for 25–30 minutes until firm to the touch and the sides have shrunk slightly away from the tin. Cool for 10 minutes and then turn out onto cooling racks until cold.

TO MAKE THE FILLING: Put the egg yolks into a medium-sized bowl and beat lightly using an electric mixer. Using a small pan dissolve the granulated sugar in the water over a gentle heat, then bring to the boil and boil rapidly, without stirring, for exactly 2 minutes. Beating very quickly, pour the syrup in a steady stream onto the yolks. Whisk at maximum speed until the mix is cool and mousse like, about 4–5 minutes.

Beat the butter in a large bowl until light. Continuing to beat, add the egg mixture a spoonful at a time, beating well after each addition. Add the sieved raspberries and stir until the mix is smooth. Add icing sugar to taste. Use half the mix to fill the cake and then spread the rest on top.

CHOCOLATE LEAVES: Using a pastry brush coat the back of each rose leaf with chocolate. Place upside down on a baking tray covered with non-stick baking parchment. When set, carefully peel off the leaves and arrange around the cake in pairs with a few in the centre.

115 g icing sugar

115 g ground almonds

4 eggs – separated

Raspberry jam

Icing sugar to dust

*22 x 32 cm swiss-roll
tin greased, lined with
baking parchment and
greased again*

*Oven temperature
170°C/325°F/Gas 3*

SWISS ROLL

Makes one cake.

Sift the icing sugar and ground almonds together twice. Beat the egg yolks with a fork.

Whisk the egg whites until very stiff. Pour the yolks over the top and mix in using a wire whisk. Sprinkle the almond mix on top and fold in lightly using a large metal spoon. Pour into the prepared tin and level the top. Bake in a pre-heated oven for 20–25 minutes until evenly browned and firm to the touch. Leave in the tin for a few minutes to cool a little.

Slide the cake out of the tin while still slightly warm and place it on the worktop, keeping the lining paper in place underneath. Peel back the edges of the paper. Using a sharp knife trim ½ cm off all around the cake.

Put the raspberry jam in a bowl and beat a little to soften. Spread over the cake. Using the lining paper lift the short edge of the cake and start to roll it, pulling the cake into a roll and peeling the paper away as the cake turns. Lift onto a serving plate and dust with icing sugar. Leave until cold before cutting.

NOTE: The cake is rolled upside down to help prevent cracking. Filling and rolling as soon as the cake is just cooled also helps, as the cake is more pliable than when completely cold.

CHOCOLATE CUP CAKES

Makes 8.

Sift ground almonds, icing sugar and cocoa together twice. Beat the yolks with the vanilla essence.

Whisk the whites until very stiff. Pour the yolks over the whites and mix thoroughly using a wire whisk. Sprinkle the almond mix over the eggs and fold in until just combined using a large metal spoon.

Divide between the cake cases and bake in a pre-heated oven for about 20 minutes until firm in the centre.

As soon as the cakes are removed from the oven place one square of chocolate in the centre of each, leave until melted and then spread over the top. May be decorated with chocolate sprinkles or grated chocolate. Leave on a cooling rack until set.

60 g ground almonds

60 g icing sugar

10 g cocoa powder

2 eggs – separated

½ tsp vanilla essence

8 small squares milk or white chocolate (see notes)

Chocolate sprinkles (see notes)

Bun tray lined with foil or paper cake cases

Oven temperature 180°C/350°F/Gas 4

BATTENBURG CAKE

85 g icing sugar

90 g ground almonds

2 tsp cocoa powder

3 eggs – separated

½ tsp vanilla essence

Sieved apricot jam

200 g marzipan
(see page 55)

Icing sugar to dust

16 x 16 cm deep cake tin, greased, lined with baking parchment and greased again. Crease the parchment in the middle to form a raised wall to divide the pan in two

Oven temperature 170°C/325°F/Gas 3

Makes one cake.

Sift the icing sugar and ground almonds together twice. Measure out 95 g of the sifted mixture and set aside. Add the cocoa to the remainder and sift again. Beat the egg yolks and essence together.

Whisk the whites until very stiff. Pour the yolk mix over the whites and fold in using a wire whisk. Divide the mixture in two. Add the plain almond mix to one half and carefully combine using a metal spoon. Spoon into one half of the prepared tin – use a cup or glass in the empty half to prop the wall up.

Add the cocoa mix to the other half and fold in as before. Spoon into the empty half of the tin and level the tops. The cocoa side may be a little lower at this stage.

Bake in a pre-heated oven for 30–40 minutes until firm to the touch and the cake has shrunk away from the sides a little. Don't worry if the two sides are different heights – when they are stacked they will be level.

Cool in the tin for a few minutes, then carefully turn out onto a cooling rack and peel off the paper. Leave until cold.

TO FINISH: Using a sharp knife, trim the cakes to make an even shape. Stack one cake on top of the other and check they are the same length and width. Remove the top cake and cut each in half lengthways. Brush the inner sides with jam and stick one plain piece alongside a cocoa piece. Repeat with the remaining two pieces, alternating the colours. Brush the top of one set with jam and stick the second layer on top to make a chequer-board design.

Sprinkle the worktop with a little sifted icing sugar and roll out the marzipan to a rectangle large enough to wrap around the cake. Evenly brush the marzipan with sieved jam. Put the cake at one end and wrap the marzipan around, sealing the join smoothly on the lower edge. Trim each end to neaten. Crimp the top edges between finger and thumb and score the top lightly in a diamond pattern with a sharp knife. Sift over a little icing sugar and brush off the excess, leaving enough in the scores to highlight the pattern.

160 g icing sugar	
200 g ground almonds	
Grated rind of 2 oranges	
5 eggs – separated	
½ tsp vanilla essence	

ICING

130 g sifted icing sugar

Juice of 1 orange

10–12 physalis (Cape Gooseberries)

23 cm diameter ring cake tin, well greased and dusted as instructed in the recipe

Oven temperature 170°C/325°F/Gas 3

ORANGE RING CAKE

Makes one cake to serve 8–10.

Sift the icing sugar and ground almonds together twice. Use two teaspoons of this mixture to dust the greased tin, knocking any surplus back into the bowl. Mix the orange rind evenly throughout the almonds. Mix the egg yolks with the vanilla essence.

Whisk egg whites until very stiff. Pour the yolks over and mix well using a wire whisk. Sprinkle the almond mix over and fold in lightly using a large metal spoon. Pour into the prepared tin and bake in a pre-heated oven for 25–30 minutes or until the cake is cooked and firm. The centre may sink a little towards the end of the baking time but it won't matter.

Cool for 10 minutes in the tin then carefully turn out onto a piece of non-stick baking parchment and then leave on a rack until cold. Slide the cake onto a serving plate.

ICING: Mix the icing sugar with just enough orange juice to make a thick icing. Reserve 2 tblsp and spread the remainder around the top of the cake, allowing it to run down the sides a little. Peel back the papery covering of the fruit, giving each one a little twist to make them hold their shape. Dip the fruit in the reserved icing and arrange around the cake.

LAYERED LEMON SQUARES

If you love the taste of lemon curd and are on the lookout for a new way to enjoy it then these are perfect – easy to make, delicious and tangy! Makes 8 squares.

Sift the icing sugar and almonds together twice. Beat the yolks with a fork.

Whisk the egg whites until very stiff. Pour the yolks over the top and mix thoroughly using a wire whisk. Sprinkle the almond mix on top and fold in using a large metal spoon. Spoon into the prepared tin and smooth the top. Bake in a pre-heated oven for about 20–25 minutes until evenly browned and firm to the touch. Cool in the tin.

Turn out onto a sheet of greaseproof paper and peel off base paper. Keeping the underside as the top throughout use a sharp knife to cut into three equal pieces of about 22 x 11 cm.

FILLING AND ICING: Spread one layer with lemon curd. Stack another layer on top and spread with more lemon curd. Add the last layer. Mix the icing sugar with a little lemon juice. Spread over the top and sprinkle over the lemon rind.

Leave to set then cut into eight squares.

100 g icing sugar

115 g ground almonds

4 eggs – separated

FILLING & ICING

Lemon curd – starch-free

120 g sifted icing sugar

Finely pared rind and juice of 1 lemon

33 x 22 cm swiss-roll tin greased, lined with baking parchment and greased again

Oven temperature 170°C/325°F/Gas 3

SACHERTORTE

150 g dark chocolate
(see notes)

120 g soft unsalted butter

115 g caster sugar

5 eggs – separated

½ tsp vanilla essence

160 g ground almonds

TOPPING

6 tblsp apricot conserve

175 g dark chocolate
(see notes)

120 ml double cream

1 tblsp butter

20 g milk chocolate
(see notes)

23 cm springform or loose-based sandwich tin, greased, base-lined and greased again

Oven temperature
170°C/325°F/Gas 3

Makes one 23 cm cake.

Melt the chocolate. Beat the butter and sugar until the mixture is light and fluffy. Mix the egg yolks with the essence and add a little at a time, beating well after each addition. Stirring all the time pour in the chocolate and mix very thoroughly. Stir in the almonds.

Whisk the egg whites until very stiff. Using a wire whisk mix ¼ of the whites into the mixture to lighten it. Add the remaining egg whites in two or three batches, stirring just enough to combine. Pour into the prepared tin. Chill for 25 minutes.

Bake in a pre-heated oven for 40–45 minutes until the cake is firm in the centre. Leave to cool in the tin for 20 minutes then turn out onto a rack. Leave until cold then place on a serving plate.

TO MAKE THE TOPPING: Spread the apricot conserve over the top. Break the dark chocolate into a bowl. Heat the cream and butter until just boiling and pour over the chocolate, stirring **very gently** until smooth, if necessary warming the mixture slightly to melt the chocolate. Chill, without stirring, until the mixture starts to thicken. Pour over the cake, smoothing the mixture down over the sides. Leave to set.

Melt the milk chocolate and put into a small freezer bag. Snip off the corner and pipe the word 'Sacher' across the centre of the cake.

This cake is best made a day or so before eating. It is very rich so serve in small slices as a dessert, or with tea or coffee.

| 100 g dried cherries |
| 300 g currants |
| 150 g sultanas |
| 150 g raisins |
| 100 g chopped candied peel (see recipe on page 156) |
| Grated rind of 1 orange |
| Grated rind of 1 lemon |
| 100 g chopped almonds |
| 6 tblsp orange juice |
| 6 tblsp brandy |
| 200 g ground almonds |
| 175 g soft brown sugar |
| 4 eggs – separated |
| 1 tsp vanilla essence |
| 1 tsp almond essence |

CHRISTMAS CAKE

This cake is very easily and quickly prepared with no risk of the mix curdling. As this recipe doesn't contain any butter it is better made shortly before eating. Makes one 18 cm square, or one 20 cm round, cake.

Mix the cherries, currants, sultanas, raisins, peel, rinds and chopped almonds in a large glass or china bowl. Mix the orange juice and brandy together and pour over the dried fruits, stirring well. Cover and leave for several hours, stirring occasionally, until the fruit has absorbed the liquid.

Sift the almonds and sugar together twice. Mix egg yolks with the essences. Whisk the egg whites until very stiff. Pour the yolks over and mix well together using a wire whisk. Pour the fruit mix on top and stir together. Sprinkle the almond mix on top and stir together using a large metal spoon.

Spoon into the prepared tin and level the top. There is no need to make a dip in the centre as the cake comes out the same size as it goes in. Fold two sheets of newspaper into a band and tie around the outside of the tin. Stand the tin in the oven on another two sheets of folded newspaper. Bake in a pre-heated oven for 3–3½ hours until a skewer inserted in the centre comes out clean. If the top starts to brown too much cover with a piece of baking parchment. Cool in the tin. Turn out and place on a serving plate or silver board.

MARZIPAN LAYER: *Makes 800 g to generously cover an 18–20 cm cake.*

Mix the almonds with the caster and icing sugar. Mix ¾ of the egg whites with the essence, lemon juice and brandy if using. Add to the almonds and sugar and stir to make a stiff but pliable mixture, adding more egg white if necessary. Knead lightly until smooth. Brush the sides of the cake with jam. Dust the work surface with icing sugar and roll out two thirds of the marzipan into a strip long enough to wrap around the cake. Press into place. Brush the top of the cake with jam and roll out the remaining marzipan until large enough to cover the top. Press into place and neaten the joins, using a little jam to stick the edges together if necessary. Leave for a day to dry before covering with icing.

ICING: *Sufficient to rough ice an 18–20 cm cake.*

Beat the egg whites until slightly frothy. Add half the icing sugar and the lemon juice and beat well until smooth and glossy. Add half the remaining icing sugar and beat well. Add the rest of the icing sugar gradually until a stiff mixture is obtained that holds its peaks when pulled with the back of a spoon. Reserve 2 tblsp of the icing and put into a sealed container. Put the remaining icing on top of the cake and use a knife to smooth it down over the sides to cover the marzipan completely. When evenly coated use the back of a metal spoon to pull soft peaks over the cake. Leave to set.

Decorate the cake with a ribbon and chocolate decorations, held in place with the reserved icing. Dust lightly with icing sugar (optional).

MARZIPAN

400 g ground almonds

200 g caster sugar

200 g sifted icing sugar

2 egg whites – mixed with a fork

1 tsp almond essence

1 tsp lemon juice

1 tsp brandy – optional

Sieved apricot jam

ICING

4 egg whites

900 g sifted icing sugar

2 tsp lemon juice

Chocolate decorations (see notes) and ribbon to finish

18 cm square or 20 cm round deep cake tin, base and sides greased and lined with a double thickness of baking parchment, then greased again

Oven temperature 150°C/300°F/Gas 2

CHOCOLATE SQUARES

5 eggs – separated

1 tsp vanilla essence

140 g ground almonds

140 g icing sugar

20 g cocoa powder

ICING

4 tsp cocoa dissolved in a
little hot water

300 g sifted icing sugar

4 large Cadbury Flakes, or
other crumbly chocolate bars
(see notes) – cut into pieces

*20 x 24 cm cake tin,
greased, lined with
baking parchment and
greased again*

*Oven temperature
170°C/325°F/Gas 3*

Makes 20 small cakes.

Mix egg yolks with a fork until well blended and stir in vanilla essence. Sift ground almonds, icing sugar and cocoa together twice.

Whisk egg whites until very stiff. Pour the yolks over and mix together thoroughly using a wire whisk. Sprinkle the almond mixture over the top and gently fold together using a large metal spoon. Pour into the prepared tin and level the top.

Bake in a pre-heated oven for about 30 minutes until firm to the touch. Cool for a few minutes in the tin and then turn out onto a cooling rack until cold.

TO FINISH: Place cake upside down on a cutting board and trim to neaten edges. Cut into 20 even-sized pieces. Place on a rack, leaving the pieces upside down so they are flat when iced.

Mix the dissolved cocoa into the icing sugar, adding a little more hot water if necessary to make a coating consistency. Working on one cake at a time drop a teaspoonful of icing onto the top and spread down over the sides to coat evenly. Add a piece of chocolate to the top and leave on the rack until set and dry. Put into paper cases to serve.

SPONGE FINGERS

Makes about 20.

Sift the ground almonds twice. Whisk egg whites until stiff. Whisk in the icing sugar a spoonful at a time, whisking until it resembles meringue. Fold the almonds into the mixture using a metal spoon, mixing well.

Spoon into a forcing bag fitted with a 1.3 cm plain nozzle. Pipe fingers 1.5 x 9 cm onto the prepared baking trays. Sift a little icing sugar on top of each finger and leave to stand for a minute.

Bake in a pre-heated oven for 15–20 minutes until lightly browned and firm on the outside but still soft inside. Transfer on the parchment to a cooling rack and leave until cold. Carefully peel off the parchment and store the fingers in an airtight tin.

Dust with a little icing sugar and serve with fruit desserts, or alternatively use as the base in trifles.

60 g ground almonds

3 egg whites

90 g sifted icing sugar

Baking trays lined with baking parchment and dusted with icing sugar

Oven temperature 170°C/325°F/Gas 3

SIMNEL CAKE

300 g currants

180 g sultanas

100 g dried cranberries

Grated rind of 1 lemon
and 1 orange

Juice of 1 orange and
1 lemon

200 g ground almonds

160 g soft brown sugar

4 eggs – separated

500 g marzipan
(see page 55)

Sieved apricot jam

*20 cm loose-based cake tin,
base and sides greased,
lined with a double thickness
of baking parchment, then
greased again*

*Oven temperature
150°C/300°F/Gas 2*

This is traditionally eaten on Mothering Sunday but is now more usually made as an Easter cake. Makes one 20 cm round cake.

Put the currants, sultanas, cranberries and orange and lemon rind in a china or glass bowl. Pour over the juices, stir well and leave to soak for three or four hours or overnight.

Sift the ground almonds and sugar together twice. Beat the egg yolks with a fork.

Roll out one third of the marzipan to a circle the size of the tin. Leave aside.

Whisk the egg whites until very stiff. Pour the yolks over the top and mix thoroughly using a wire whisk. Add the fruit mix and stir in. Sprinkle the almond mix on top and fold in using a large metal spoon. Put half the mixture in the prepared tin and level the top. Place the circle of marzipan over the cake mix. Add the remaining cake mix and smooth top.

Fold a sheet of newspaper into a band and tie around the tin. Stand the tin on a couple of sheets of folded newspaper in the oven and bake in a pre-heated oven for 3–3½ hours until evenly browned, firm to the touch, and a skewer inserted in the centre comes out clean. Cover the top of the cake with a circle of baking paper if it starts to brown too much.

Leave to cool in the tin. When cold, peel off the paper and place the cake on a grill pan.

Cut off ¼ of the remaining marzipan and shape into 11 even-sized balls. Roll out the rest of the marzipan to fit the top of the cake. Brush the top of the cake with a little jam and stick the marzipan in place. Stick the balls around the edge, evenly spaced, using a little jam. Brush a little jam over the top and place under a pre-heated grill until just browned.

Tie a pretty ribbon around the cake before serving.

MINI CHOCOLATE KOUGELHOPFS

6 eggs – separated

1 tsp vanilla essence

250 g ground almonds

190 g icing sugar

30 g cocoa powder

50 g milk chocolate chips
(see notes)

ICING

120 g sifted icing sugar.

40 g milk chocolate (see
notes) – melted

*6 non-stick mini kougelhopf
tins (approx 240 ml in
size), well greased with
melted butter*

*Oven temperature
170°C/325°F/Gas 3*

Makes 6.

Mix the egg yolks and vanilla essence together. Sift the ground almonds, the icing sugar and the cocoa powder together twice. Stir in the milk chocolate chips.

Whisk the egg whites until very stiff. Pour the yolks over the whites and use a wire whisk to mix thoroughly. Sprinkle the almond mixture over the egg mix and fold in using a large metal spoon.

Spoon the mixture into the prepared tins, making sure the mix goes right into the base. Smooth the tops. Bake in a pre-heated oven for about 25 minutes until the cakes are cooked and firm to the touch. Cool in the tins for 10 minutes and then turn out onto a cooling rack until cold.

TO MAKE THE ICING: Mix the icing sugar with just enough cold water to make a thick glacé icing. Spoon around the tops of the cakes allowing the icing to run down over the sides a little. Leave until set. Put the melted chocolate in the corner of a small freezer bag, snip off a tiny piece from the corner and drizzle over the icing.

CHOCOLATE & HAZELNUT TORTE

4 eggs – separated

125 g caster sugar

125 g ground hazelnuts

FILLING AND TOPPING

120 g soft unsalted butter

120 g icing sugar

60 g dark chocolate (see notes) – melted

1 tblsp chopped toasted hazelnuts

8 whole hazelnuts

Two 18 cm loose-based sandwich cake tins, greased, base-lined and greased again

Oven temperature 170°C/325°F/Gas 3

Makes one 18 cm cake to serve 8.

Beat the egg yolks and caster sugar together until well blended and light. Then beat in the ground hazelnuts.

Whisk egg whites until very stiff. Fold ¼ of the whites into the nut mixture to lighten. Fold in the remaining whites in three batches, mixing just enough to make an even mixture. Divide between the tins and level the tops.

Bake in a pre-heated oven for about 25 minutes until firm in the centre. Cool for a few minutes in the tins and then turn out onto cooling racks and peel off the paper.

TO MAKE THE FILLING: Beat the butter and icing sugar together until light and fluffy. Beat in the melted chocolate.

Put a little less than ⅓ of the mixture in a piping bag fitted with a large star tube. Use half of the remaining icing to sandwich the cakes together, and the rest to coat the top. Sprinkle the chopped toasted hazelnuts over the top. Pipe eight rosettes around the edge of the cake and place a whole hazelnut on the top of each rosette. Leave to set.

YULE LOG

130 g icing sugar

100 g ground almonds

20 g cocoa

4 eggs – separated

½ tsp coffee granules

½ tsp boiling water

FILLING AND ICING

150 g soft unsalted butter

300 g sifted icing sugar

½ tsp vanilla essence

150 g milk chocolate
(see notes) – melted

4 large Cadbury Flakes, or
other crumbly chocolate bars
(see notes)

Icing sugar to sprinkle

*32 x 22 cm swiss-roll tin,
greased, fully lined with
baking parchment, then
greased again*

*Oven temperature
170°C/325°F/Gas 3*

Makes one cake.

Sift the icing sugar, ground almonds and cocoa together twice, making sure they are well mixed. Beat the egg yolks with a fork. Dissolve the coffee in the boiling water and then beat into the yolks.

Whisk the egg whites until very stiff. Pour the yolks over the top and mix in thoroughly using a wire whisk. Sprinkle the almond mix on top and fold in using a large metal spoon. Spoon into the prepared tin and level the top. Bake in a pre-heated oven for 20–25 minutes until firm to the touch. Leave in the tin until just cool.

TO MAKE THE FILLING: Beat the butter until pale, then beat in the icing sugar and the essence and continue beating until light and fluffy. Add the melted milk chocolate and beat well.

Slide the barely cool cake out onto the worktop, keeping the lining paper in place underneath. Peel back the edges of the paper. Use a very sharp knife to trim ½ cm from the cake edges and then spread with half the filling. Using the paper, lift the short edge of the cake and start to roll it, pulling the paper away as it turns.

Using a sharp knife, cut an angled wedge from one end – about 1½ cm at the shortest side and about 3 cm at the longest side – and stick in place with a little icing to represent a branch on the side of the yule log.

ICING: Cover the cake with the remaining icing. Cut the chocolate bars lengthways into strips and press into the icing to represent bark. Use a skewer to mark the ends of the log and the branch to represent rings. Put a little icing sugar in a sieve and dust the log to represent snow. Add a sprig of holly to serve.

NOTE: The cake is rolled upside down to help prevent cracking. Filling and rolling as soon as the cake is just cooled also helps, as the cake is more pliable than when completely cold.

MOCHA BUNS

2 tsp coffee granules

1 tsp boiling water

3 eggs – separated

100 g ground almonds

100 g icing sugar

1½ tsp cocoa

ICING

100 g icing sugar.

1 tsp coffee granules dissolved in a little hot water.

12 chocolate-covered coffee beans (see notes)

Bun tray lined with cup cake cases

Oven temperature 180°C/350°F/Gas 4

Makes 12.

Dissolve the coffee granules in the boiling water. Beat the egg yolks with a fork and then mix in the coffee. Sift the ground almonds, icing sugar and cocoa twice.

Whisk the egg whites until very stiff. Pour the egg yolk mixture over the top and mix in thoroughly using a wire whisk. Sprinkle the almond mix over and fold in using a large metal spoon. Divide the mixture between the paper cases and bake in a pre-heated oven for about 20 minutes until firm in the centre. Cool on a rack.

ICING: Mix the icing sugar with just enough dissolved coffee to make a spreadable icing. Spoon a little icing onto each bun and top with a coffee bean.

EASTER NESTS

Makes 6.

Sift the ground almonds, icing sugar and cocoa together twice. Mix the egg yolks with the essence, mixing well with a fork.

Whisk the whites until very stiff. Pour the yolks over the top and mix together using a wire whisk until well combined. Sprinkle the almond mix over the top and lightly fold together using a large metal spoon until just mixed.

Divide the mixture between the paper muffin cases and bake in a pre-heated oven for 15–20 minutes until firm to the touch. Transfer to a cooling rack until cold.

TO MAKE THE TOPPING: Dissolve the cocoa in a small amount of hot water. Mix the icing sugar with the dissolved cocoa. Beat in the butter a little at a time. Beat until smooth. Mix in the grated chocolate. Divide the topping between the cakes, using a fork to roughen the surface to represent a nest. Put a chocolate egg in the centre of each.

60 g ground almonds

60 g icing sugar

2 tsp cocoa powder

2 eggs – separated

Few drops vanilla essence

TOPPING

2 tsp cocoa powder

70 g icing sugar – sifted

30 g soft unsalted butter

20 g grated chocolate
(see notes)

Chocolate eggs to finish
(see notes)

Paper muffin cases in a muffin tray, or placed doubled up on a baking tray to hold the shape

Oven temperature 180°C/350°F/Gas 4

BLUEBERRY HEARTS

2 eggs – separated

60 g icing sugar

90 g ground almonds

75 g dried blueberries

Icing sugar to finish

6 non-stick heart-shaped tins,
approximately 9 cm wide,
well greased

Oven temperature
170°C/325°F/Gas 3

These little cakes can be whipped up in minutes. Serve them lightly dusted with icing sugar for a quick and easy coffee-time treat. Makes 6.

Beat the egg yolks with a fork. Sift the icing sugar and ground almonds together twice. Stir in the blueberries.

Whisk the egg whites until very stiff. Pour the yolks over the top and mix together using a wire whisk. Sprinkle the almond mixture on top and fold in using a large metal spoon.

Spoon into the prepared tins and smooth the tops. Bake in a pre-heated oven for about 20 minutes until firm to the touch and nicely browned. Turn out onto a cooling rack and sift a little icing sugar over the top. Leave until cold.

VARIATION: For a design on the top of the cakes place three or four chopsticks on top before sifting the icing sugar over the top. Repeat for each cake.

NOTE: If heart-shaped tins are unavailable, the mixture can be baked in paper cake cases or well-greased bun tins instead. Check halfway through the cooking time as smaller cakes will cook more quickly.

ICED SPONGE

This is a pretty little cake that's easy to make. For an even simpler version sandwich the cakes together with jam and sift icing sugar on top. Makes one 18 cm cake.

Beat the egg yolks with a fork. Sift the icing sugar and ground almonds together twice.

Whisk the egg whites until very stiff. Pour the yolks over the top and mix thoroughly using a wire whisk. Sprinkle the almond mix on top and fold in using a large metal spoon.

Divide between the tins, leaving the centres a little higher. Bake in a pre-heated oven for about 25 minutes or until firm to the touch and cooked through. Leave to cool in the tins for 5 minutes. Remove the outer rings and slide the cakes off the bases onto a cooling rack, keeping the cooking paper underneath. Leave until cold.

TO FINISH: Choose one cake for the base and spread with 3 tblsp jam. Invert the other cake on top and remove the paper. Keeping the cake on the base paper for ease of handling, spread the remaining jam evenly around the side. Spread the coconut on a plate and roll the cake in the coconut to coat evenly. Place on a serving plate, still on the paper base if preferred.

Beat the butter until soft and then beat in the icing sugar and vanilla essence. Add a little water if necessary to make a soft piping icing. Fit an icing bag with a small star nozzle and fill with icing. Pipe small stars all over the top, starting at the centre.

NOTE: To toast coconut, put desiccated coconut in an even layer in a shallow tin. Bake for 5–10 minutes at 150°C/300°F/Gas 2, stirring once or twice, until lightly browned.

---

4 eggs – separated

120 g icing sugar

180 g ground almonds

FILLING AND ICING

5 tblsp raspberry jam

25 g desiccated coconut – toasted

60 g unsalted butter

140 g sifted icing sugar

½ tsp vanilla essence

1–2 tsp hot water

Two 18 cm loose-based cake tins, greased, base-lined and greased again

Oven temperature 170°C/325°F/Gas 3

BISCUITS & BARS

Who doesn't enjoy the occasional Choc-Chip Cookie? Or a piece of Millionaires' Shortbread with that gorgeous layer of fudgy toffee covered in chocolate? Or a Coconut Biscuit? Or a Walnut Brownie? There's something rather comforting about a couple of crunchy biscuits with a cup of coffee, or a piece of date bar for afternoon tea. In this chapter there is a selection of some of the most popular biscuits, which are all very easy to make and bake. These biscuits are particularly good for taking when travelling – a few in a small container make a great standby for outings when you aren't sure what snacks will be available. They look and taste just as good as the ones they replace, so don't be surprised if you get some disbelieving looks when you say they are flour-free.

You can never tell on your first one ...

DATE BARS

FILLING

250 g chopped dates

1 tblsp soft brown sugar

1 tblsp lemon juice

4–5 tblsp water

BASE AND TOPPING

300 g ground almonds

120 g icing sugar

1 tsp finely grated
lemon rind

120 g soft unsalted butter,
diced

*Baking tin 24 x 20 cm,
greased, lined with
baking parchment, and
greased again*

*Oven temperature
170°C/325°F/Gas 3*

*These are every bit as good as the regular ones – just a little softer. Makes
about 16 bars or squares.*

Put all the filling ingredients into a saucepan and heat gently, stirring well
until smooth.

Put the ground almonds, icing sugar and lemon rind into a bowl, add the
butter and gently rub in until the mixture resembles coarse breadcrumbs.
Remove half for the topping and knead the remainder to a dough.

Place a sheet of all-purpose food wrap on the worktop, place the dough on
top and cover with a piece of greaseproof paper or non-stick parchment.
Press or roll out to the size of the tin. Peel off the paper and invert the dough,
still on the food wrap, into the lined tin, pressing and smoothing to fit. Peel
off the food wrap.

Bake the base in a pre-heated oven for 10 minutes to pre-cook it. Carefully
spoon the date mixture on top in an even layer, being careful not to tear
the dough. Sprinkle over the remaining mixture in an even layer and press
lightly to firm.

Bake for about 20 minutes more, until nicely browned. Cut into bars or
squares while still warm, but leave in the tin until cold.

COCONUT BISCUITS

Makes 20.

Beat butter, sugar and egg yolk together until light and creamy.

Mix the ground almonds, coconut, baking powder and orange rind together. Stir into the creamed mixture, adding enough egg white to make a firm dough.

Put the coconut and caster sugar mixture on a small plate. Form the biscuit mix into 20 even-sized balls. Flatten into neat rounds and press the tops into the coconut and caster sugar mixture. Place on the prepared trays.

Bake in a pre-heated oven for about 15 minutes until lightly browned, turning the trays as necessary to cook evenly. Leave on the trays for a couple of minutes and then transfer to cooling racks until cold and crisp.

50 g soft unsalted butter

100 g caster sugar

1 egg yolk

110 g ground almonds

90 g desiccated coconut

½ tsp baking powder
(see notes)

Grated rind of 1 orange

1–2 tsp beaten egg white

1½ tblsp desiccated coconut mixed with 1 ½ tblsp caster sugar to finish

Non-stick baking trays, greased

*Oven temperature
150°C/300°F/Gas 2*

GINGER BISCUIT PEOPLE

100 g unsalted butter

100 g light brown muscovado sugar

1 egg yolk

1½–2 tsp ginger essence

180 g ground almonds

Currants to decorate

Non-stick baking trays, greased

Oven temperature 170°C/325°F/Gas 3

This recipe uses ginger essence instead of ground ginger, which doesn't agree with me. If you prefer use 1–2 tsp ground ginger instead. Makes about 20, depending on the size of the cutters used.

Beat butter and sugar until pale. Beat in egg yolk and essence. Stir in almonds and knead lightly. Place a piece of greaseproof paper or baking parchment on the worktop, place the biscuit dough on top and cover with a piece of all-purpose food wrap.

Roll out between the paper and food wrap to a ½ – ¾ cm thickness. Peel off food wrap and lightly sprinkle the dough with a little extra ground almonds. Turn over onto the worktop and peel off the paper. Cut out shapes and place on the prepared baking trays. Press currants into the dough to represent eyes and buttons. Re-roll trimmings as before.

Bake in a pre-heated oven for about 10–12 minutes until lightly browned. Cool on the trays for a couple of minutes and then transfer to a cooling rack until cold and crisp.

CHOC–CHIP COOKIES

Makes 20. (Also see photograph on page 68.)

Beat butter and sugar well. Mix egg yolk with essence and beat into butter mix. Stir in almonds and chocolate chips and mix to a firm dough.

Form into 20 balls. Place them well spaced apart on the prepared baking trays and flatten them into neat rounds. Bake in a pre-heated oven for 10–12 minutes until nicely browned, turning the trays if necessary to ensure even browning.

Cool on the trays for a minute and then use a fish slice or large-bladed knife to transfer the biscuits to a cooling rack. Leave until cold and crisp.

100 g unsalted butter

100 g caster sugar

1 egg yolk

1 tsp vanilla essence

150 g ground almonds

100 g chocolate chips
(see notes)

Non-stick baking trays, greased

*Oven temperature
180°C/350°F/Gas 4*

CHOCOLATE ORANGE DROPS

40 g ground almonds

4 egg whites

160 g sifted icing sugar

1 tsp vanilla essence

80 g orange flavoured dark chocolate (see notes)

Baking trays lined with baking parchment and sprinkled with icing sugar

Oven temperature 170°C/325°F/Gas 3

Makes about 40.

Sift the ground almonds. Whisk the egg whites to soft peaks, add the icing sugar and whisk until stiff. Stir in the essence. Fold in the ground almonds.

Spoon the mixture into a forcing bag fitted with a plain 1.3 cm nozzle. Keeping the bag upright, pipe rounds onto the prepared baking trays. Sieve a little icing sugar over the top of each round and leave for a minute or two until most of the sugar has dissolved.

Bake in a pre-heated oven for 15–20 minutes until lightly browned and firm to the touch. The inside should still be soft. Lift the paper onto a cooling rack, leave until cold and then carefully peel off the paper.

Melt the chocolate. Working one at a time, spoon a little chocolate onto the base of a biscuit and smooth evenly to the edges. Leave upside down on a cooling rack until set. Place in an airtight tin in a cool place. Serve with coffee as an after-dinner sweet.

ALMOND ROCKS

These lovely squidgy meringues are crisp on the outside and deliciously gooey inside. Makes 15.

Whisk egg whites until stiff. Whisk in the sugar a tablespoon at a time. Stir in the almonds and the essence. Place in mounds on the prepared trays, spacing well apart.

Bake in a pre-heated oven for 30–35 minutes until lightly browned. Transfer to cooling racks and leave until cold.

Melt the chocolate and pour into a small freezer bag, snip off the corner and drizzle the chocolate over the rocks. Leave to set.

2 egg whites

115 g caster sugar

150 g flaked almonds

Few drops almond essence

40 g chocolate (see notes)

Baking trays lined with baking parchment

Oven temperature 150°C/300°F/Gas 2

MILLIONAIRES' SHORTBREAD

BASE

125 g ground almonds

50 g caster sugar

50 g unsalted butter

CARAMEL LAYER

1 x 400 g tin of
condensed milk

55 g soft brown sugar

55 g unsalted butter

½ tsp vanilla essence

TOPPING

100 g dark, milk or white
chocolate (see notes)

*Baking tin 20 x 24 cm,
greased, lined with
baking parchment
and greased again*

*Oven temperature
150°C/300°F/Gas 2*

*A delicious shortbread layer with a thick caramel filling and chocolate
topping. Very easy to make and great for snacks. Makes 16 squares.*

Mix the almonds and caster sugar together and then rub the butter in,
distributing it through the almonds with your fingers. Knead lightly until a
dough is formed.

Pull off pieces of dough and scatter over the base of the prepared tin. Press
down until the base of the tin is covered, then use the back of a spoon to
smooth the dough into an even layer.

Bake in a pre-heated oven for about 15 minutes or until lightly browned.
Cool in the tin.

FOR THE CARAMEL LAYER: Place all the ingredients in a pan and
heat gently until the sugar is melted. Bring to a simmer and then cook
gently, stirring all the time with a wooden spatula, until the mixture
thickens. This will take about 6–7 minutes. Pour over the cooled shortbread
mixture, smooth the surface and leave to cool and set.

FOR THE TOPPING: Melt chocolate. Pour over the caramel layer and
smooth the top. Leave to set, then chill before cutting into squares.

VARIATION: Use 50 g milk chocolate and 50 g of white chocolate.
Place them in alternating spoonfuls on the top and swirl together to create
a marbled appearance.

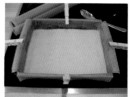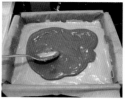

HAZELNUT BISCUITS

150 g ground almonds

100 g caster sugar

100 g chopped roasted hazelnuts

100 g unsalted butter – diced

Non-stick baking trays, greased

Oven temperature 180°C/350°F/Gas 4

Makes 20.

Mix almonds, sugar and about ¾ of the hazelnuts together, reserving enough hazelnuts for the top of the biscuits. Rub the butter into the mix and knead by hand to a firm dough.

Divide into 20 even-sized pieces, roll into balls and flatten into neat rounds on the baking trays. Top with the reserved hazelnuts, lightly pressing them into the dough.

Bake in a pre-heated oven for 8–10 minutes or until nicely browned. Cool for a minute or two on the trays and then carefully transfer to cooling racks until cold and crisp.

MACADAMIA & WHITE CHOCOLATE COOKIES

Makes 18–20.

Beat butter and sugar well. Mix egg yolk with essence and beat in. Mix almonds with the chopped chocolate and nuts and stir into mixture, kneading to make a firm dough.

Form into 18–20 balls. Place them well spaced apart on the prepared baking trays and flatten them into neat rounds.

Bake in a pre-heated oven for 10–12 minutes until very lightly browned. Allow to cool for a minute and then use a fish slice to transfer to cooling racks until cold and crisp.

100 g unsalted butter

110 g caster sugar

1 egg yolk

1 tsp vanilla essence

150 g ground almonds

50 g white chocolate (see notes) – chopped

50 g macadamia nuts – chopped

Non-stick baking trays, greased

Oven temperature 180°C/350°F/Gas 4

BRANDY SNAPS

30 g unsalted butter

90 g caster sugar

15 ml golden syrup

½ tsp ginger essence

25 g ground almonds –
weighed after sifting

Whipped cream to serve
(optional)

*Non-stick baking trays,
lightly greased. 18 cm
diameter baking-parchment
circles*

*Oven temperature
180°C/350°F/Gas 4*

These work brilliantly, with none of the usual difficulty removing the biscuits from the baking trays. These use ginger essence instead of ground ginger. If the starch in the ginger isn't a problem for you, use ½ tsp ground ginger if you prefer. Makes 10.

Using an electric mixer if possible, beat butter and sugar until light and fluffy. Beat in syrup and essence. Add almonds and stir in. Knead lightly until smooth and then form into 10 even-sized balls. Flatten between your fingers to fat discs about 4 cm in diameter.

Lightly grease three parchment discs and space them evenly on a baking tray. Place a disc of dough in the centre of each paper. Bake one tray at a time in a pre-heated oven for 7–9 minutes, until the mixture has spread and the biscuit is a good golden brown all over. Turn the tray around if necessary to ensure even cooking. Watch carefully as it only takes a few seconds for the biscuits to overcook.

Take the tray from the oven, leave the biscuits for a minute to firm up, then lift the biscuit on the parchment and place upside down on another parchment disc on the worktop. They should be just cool enough to handle but still pliable. Peel off the cooking parchment and roll the biscuit around the greased handle of a wooden spoon. As soon as it is set, slide it off and repeat with the other biscuits. A second tray can be baking as you roll the first ones. If the biscuits become too firm to roll return the tray to the oven for a few seconds to soften.

Store the biscuits in an airtight container as soon as they have cooled. Serve as they are or fill with a little whipped cream.

The snaps can also be shaped over a greased upturned cup to make baskets for fruit or ice cream. Make more than you need to allow for casualties – if some break then crush them and serve over ice cream.

NOTE: It is not essential to grease the trays but it does stop the parchment discs sliding about.

EASTER BISCUITS

100 g unsalted butter

80 g caster sugar

1 egg – separated

½ tsp almond essence

½ tsp ginger essence

Grated rind of ½ lemon – optional

60 g currants

180 g ground almonds

Caster sugar for sprinkling

Non-stick baking trays, greased

Oven temperature 150°C/300°F/Gas 2

Makes 20–24.

Beat the butter and sugar together until smooth. Beat the egg yolk and essences together with a fork and then beat them into the butter mix. Stir in the rind if using. Add the currants and ground almonds and mix together to form a dough.

Place a piece of greaseproof paper on the worktop, place the ball of dough on top and cover with a piece of all-purpose food wrap. Roll out to required thickness and peel off the food wrap. Sprinkle a little extra ground almonds over the dough, turn over onto the worktop and peel off the paper. Cut out using a 6 cm cutter and place on the prepared baking trays. Re-roll the trimmings as before.

Bake in a pre-heated oven for about 10 minutes until barely coloured but firm. Remove from the oven, carefully brush with a little beaten egg white and sprinkle with caster sugar. Bake for a further 5–7 minutes until lightly browned.

Leave for a minute or two, then carefully transfer to cooling racks until cold.

NOTE: The biscuits will be soft when freshly cooked but will crisp as they cool.

MINI CHOC-CHIP MERINGUES

2 egg whites
....

115 g caster sugar
....

150 g milk chocolate chips
(see notes)
....

*Baking trays lined with
baking parchment*

*Oven temperature
150°C/300°F/Gas 2*

Makes 30.

Whisk whites until stiff. Whisk in the sugar a tablespoon at a time. Stir in the chocolate chips.

Place teaspoonfuls of the mixture, well spaced apart, on the prepared baking trays. Bake in a pre-heated oven for 20 minutes. Transfer to cooling racks until cold.

PIPED VANILLA BISCUITS

85 g icing sugar – sifted

100 g unsalted butter

1 egg yolk

1 tsp vanilla essence

200 g ground almonds – sifted once

TO DECORATE – optional

50 g milk or white chocolate (see notes), or a little glacé icing

Grated chocolate (see notes) or toasted almonds slivers

Non-stick baking trays, greased

Biscuit press

Oven temperature 170°C/325°F/Gas 3

Makes about 50.

Beat the icing sugar with the butter until light and fluffy. Add the egg yolk and essence and beat well. Add the ground almonds and mix to make a soft but formed biscuit dough.

Fill the tube of a biscuit press and attach the desired shape-maker to the end. Form biscuits on the baking trays and bake in a pre-heated oven for 8–10 minutes until lightly browned, turning the baking trays if necessary to ensure even browning. Cool slightly on the tray and then transfer to cooling racks until cold and crisp.

TO DECORATE: Melt the chocolate and pour into the corner of a small freezer bag. Snip off the corner of the bag and drizzle the chocolate over the biscuits. If preferred, use a little glacé icing. Sprinkle with grated chocolate or toasted almond slivers.

NOTE: The success of these delicious little biscuits depends on the almonds being very finely ground. If the almonds are a little coarser the biscuits will still taste just as good and be as crisp, but they may not retain their shape so well during baking.

PIPED CHOCOLATE BISCUITS

Makes about 60 (also shown opposite).

Sift the icing sugar and mix with the butter, beating until light and fluffy. Beat in melted chocolate and then the egg yolk and essence. Add the ground almonds and mix in well to make a soft but formed biscuit dough.

Fill the tube of a biscuit press and attach the desired shape-maker to the end. Press onto baking trays and chill for 10 minutes. Bake in a pre-heated oven for 8–10 minutes, turning the baking trays if necessary to ensure even cooking. Cool slightly on the trays and then transfer to a cooling rack until cold and crisp.

TO DECORATE: Melt the chocolate and pour into a small freezer bag. Snip off the corner and drizzle over the biscuits. If preferred, coat the base of each biscuit (shown opposite). Leave to set.

NOTE: The success of these delicious little biscuits depends on the almonds being very finely ground. If the almonds are a little coarser the biscuits will still taste just as good and be as crisp, but they may not retain their shape so well during baking.

85 g icing sugar

100g unsalted butter

100 g dark chocolate (see notes) melted in a bowl over hot water and cooled

1 egg yolk

1 tsp vanilla essence

200 g ground almonds – sifted once

TO DECORATE – optional

50 g white, milk or dark chocolate (see notes)

Non-stick baking trays, greased

Biscuit press

Oven temperature 170°C/325°F/Gas 3

VANILLA HEARTS

100 g unsalted butter

80 g caster sugar

1 egg yolk

1 tsp vanilla essence

180 g ground almonds

ICING

150 g sifted icing sugar

Beaten egg white

Pink and yellow natural food colouring

½ tsp cocoa dissolved in 1 tsp water

Non-stick baking trays, greased

Oven temperature 170°C/325°F/Gas 3

Makes about 30 depending on cutter size.

Beat butter and sugar together until blended. Beat in the egg yolk and essence. Stir in the almonds, mixing well to make a dough.

Place a piece of baking parchment or greaseproof paper on the worktop, place dough on top and cover with a piece of all-purpose food wrap. Roll out to required thickness, peel off the food wrap and lightly sprinkle the dough with a little extra ground almonds. Turn the dough over onto the worktop and peel off the paper. Cut out heart-shaped biscuits and place on the prepared baking trays. Re-roll offcuts of dough as before.

Bake in a pre-heated oven for about 10–12 minutes until lightly browned. Cool for a minute on the trays and then transfer to a cooling rack and leave until cold and crisp.

TO MAKE THE ICING: Mix the icing sugar with just enough egg white to make a stiff but spreadable icing. Divide the icing into four equal portions in small bowls. Leave one portion white. Tint one pink and another yellow with a couple of drops of colouring. An easy way to do this is by dipping the handle of a small teaspoon in the colour and allowing one or two drops to run off the end of the handle. Mix a little of the cocoa paste into the last icing, adding a little more icing sugar if the mix is too runny.

Using a small knife, ice each of the biscuits with one of the colours. Put any remaining icing in the corners of small freezer bags, snip off the corner and pipe decorations on the biscuits. If preferred use piping tubes for writing. Leave to dry.

LEMON THINS

100 g unsalted butter

80 g caster sugar

1 egg yolk

1 tsp lemon essence

180 g ground almonds

Grated rind of 1 lemon

ICING – optional

8 tblsp icing sugar

1–2 tblsp lemon juice

Non-stick baking trays, greased

Oven temperature 150°C/300°F/Gas 2

Makes 24–30 depending on cutter size.

Beat butter and sugar together until well blended. Add the egg yolk and essence, mix well, then stir in the almonds and lemon rind to make a firm dough. If the dough is sticky add a little more ground almonds.

Place a piece of baking parchment or greaseproof paper on the worktop, place dough on top and cover with a piece of all-purpose food wrap. Roll out to about ½ cm thick. Peel off food wrap and lightly sprinkle surface with a little extra ground almonds. Turn over onto worktop and peel off paper. Cut out biscuits and place on prepared trays. Re-roll trimmings as before.

Bake in a pre-heated oven for 10–12 minutes until lightly browned. Cool for a minute on the trays, then transfer to a cooling rack and leave until cold and crisp.

TO ICE: Sift the icing sugar and stir in just enough lemon juice to make a spreadable icing. Ice the centre of each biscuit and leave to set.

DOUBLE CHOC-CHIP COOKIES

Makes 20.

Beat butter and icing sugar together until pale. Beat in dissolved coffee.

Sift ground almonds and cocoa together and then stir in chocolate chips. Add to butter mix to make a dough. Divide into 20 balls and place them well-spaced apart on the prepared baking trays. Flatten to make a neat biscuit shape.

Bake in pre-heated oven for 10–12 minutes, turning the trays if necessary to ensure even cooking.

Cool on the trays for a minute and then transfer to cooling racks using a large-bladed knife or fish slice. Leave until cold and crisp.

110 g soft unsalted butter

85 g icing sugar

1 small tsp coffee granules dissolved in 1 tsp hot water

150 g ground almonds

30 g cocoa powder

100 g white, milk or dark chocolate chips (see notes)

Non-stick baking trays, greased

Oven temperature 180°C/350°F/Gas 4

ALMOND BISCUITS

75 g ground almonds

50 g caster sugar

50 g unsalted butter

Few drops almond essence

50 g toasted almonds – chopped

20 g flaked almonds to decorate

Non-stick baking trays, greased

Oven temperature 180°C/350°F/Gas 4

Makes 10.

Mix ground almonds and sugar together. Rub in butter. Stir in essence and toasted almonds and knead lightly to form a dough.

Divide into 10 even-sized pieces and roll into balls. Place on the prepared baking trays, press down to make a round biscuit and neaten the edges. Sprinkle on the flaked almonds and lightly press into the dough.

Bake in a pre-heated oven for 8–10 minutes or until lightly browned. Allow to cool on the trays for 2 minutes and then carefully lift off and transfer to a cooling rack until cold and crisp.

WALNUT BROWNIES

These have a delicious fudgy texture and a perfect brownie taste. Makes 16 squares.

Melt the dark and milk chocolate together in a bowl over hot water (see notes). Sift ground almonds and cocoa together.

Beat butter, brown sugar and essence together well. Add the egg yolks and melted chocolate and beat well. Stir in the almond mixture, then stir in walnuts and chocolate chips.

Whisk the egg whites until very stiff. Add half the whisked egg whites to the chocolate mixture and stir together carefully using a large metal spoon. Carefully stir in the remaining egg white.

Spoon into the baking tin, smooth the top and bake in a pre-heated oven for about 30 minutes until the top is set. Cool before cutting into squares.

100 g dark chocolate
(see notes)

50 g milk chocolate
(see notes)

75 g ground almonds

4 tblsp cocoa

140 g soft unsalted butter

215 g soft brown sugar

½ tsp vanilla essence

2 eggs – separated

85 g walnuts – chopped

50 g milk chocolate chips
(see notes)

*Baking tin 20 x 20 cm,
5 cm deep. Greased, lined
and greased again*

*Oven temperature
170°C/325°F/Gas 3*

DESSERTS & SWEET PASTRIES

Fresh fruit will often be the first choice for dessert. But for the times when you want something a little different, either something you used to be able to eat or something for a special occasion, here are a few adaptations of old favourites. The Chocolate Fudge Walnut Tarts are delicious served with a drizzle of fresh cream, or try the Pecan Maple Pie with ice cream. At Christmas serve the richly fruited Christmas Pudding with brandy butter in the usual way, or try the utterly convincing Mince Pies. On a winter's night there are individual Baked Syrup Sponges to keep out the cold, or for a summer meal the Strawberry Shortcake makes an indulgent finale. So whether you miss the luxury of an Old-fashioned Sherry Trifle or a delicious little Fruit Tart, or perhaps just something as simple as Apple Parcels and cream, there is something in this chapter to satisfy.

Actually, I think I could manage a small piece …

FRUIT TARTS

PASTRY

115 g sifted ground almonds

15 g sifted icing sugar

40 g unsalted butter – diced

FILLING

100 g condensed milk

60 ml double cream – whipped

2 tblsp lemon juice

Grated rind of 1 lemon

TOPPING

Raspberries, strawberries, blueberries, kiwi or other soft fruit. Use one type or a selection

GLAZE

4 tblsp redcurrant jelly for red fruits, or 4 tblsp sieved apricot jam for yellow or green fruits

1 tsp lemon juice & 1 tsp water

Four 9 cm loose-based tart tins, greased and base-lined

Oven temperature 170°C/325°F/Gas 3

Makes 4 individual tarts.

Mix the ground almonds and icing sugar in a mixing bowl. Rub in the butter until the mix is like breadcrumbs and then knead gently to make a ball of dough.

Divide into four and shape each into a ball. Place a piece of all-purpose food wrap on the work surface, put one ball in the centre and cover with a piece of baking parchment or greaseproof paper. Roll the dough between the food wrap and paper until it is large enough to line a tin.

Carefully peel off the paper – this can be used for each one – and lift the dough on the food wrap and invert into the prepared tin. Leaving the food wrap in place, gently ease the dough into the base of the tin and up the sides. Peel off the food wrap, neaten the dough and trim the edge. Repeat with the remaining dough.

Bake in a pre-heated oven for about 15 minutes until evenly browned and cooked through. When cooled and firm ease out of the tins.

FILLING: Mix the condensed milk and whipped cream together, add the lemon juice and rind and stir until the mixture thickens. Spoon into the cases and smooth tops. Chill until set.

TOPPING: Arrange fruit on cream layer.

GLAZE: Heat the jelly or jam with the lemon juice and water, stirring until melted. Spoon or brush over the top of the fruits. Leave to set. These are best served on the same day.

CHOCOLATE FUDGE WALNUT TARTS

PASTRY

120 g ground almonds

20 g icing sugar

1 level tblsp cocoa

50 g unsalted butter

FILLING

30 g dark chocolate
(see notes)

40 g unsalted butter

50 g soft brown sugar

2 tblsp liquid honey

¼ tsp vanilla essence

1 egg – beaten

80 g walnut halves

*Four 9 cm loose-based tart
tins, greased and base-lined*

*Oven temperature
150°C/300°F/Gas 2*

Makes 4 individual tarts.

TO MAKE THE PASTRY: Sift the almonds, icing sugar and cocoa together. Rub in the butter and knead until it just forms a dough. Divide into 4.

Place a sheet of all-purpose food wrap on the worktop, put a piece of the dough on top and cover with a piece of baking parchment or greaseproof paper. Roll out to a circle just big enough to line a tin. Peel off the top layer of paper and upturn the dough, on the food wrap, into a tin. Ease the dough into the base and up the sides, peel off the food wrap and neaten pastry and edge. Repeat with remaining dough, re-using the paper.

Prick base lightly with a fork and bake in a pre-heated oven for about 12 minutes until the pastry has firmed and is lightly cooked.

TO MAKE THE FILLING: Gently heat the chocolate, butter, sugar and honey together until just melted. Add the vanilla essence and egg and mix well. Divide the walnuts between the cases, taking care not to damage the pastry. Spoon the filling over the top.

Bake for about 30 minutes until the filling is set. Cool in the tins for 10 minutes and then carefully turn out. Serve warm or cold with cream.

JAM TARTS

Makes 12.

Sift the ground almonds and the icing sugar together. Rub in the butter until the mixture resembles breadcrumbs and knead lightly to form a dough.

Place a piece of greaseproof paper on the worktop, place the dough on top and cover with a piece of all-purpose food wrap or another piece of greaseproof paper. Roll out between the papers to an even thickness of a little over ½ cm. Peel off the top paper. Lightly sprinkle the top of the pastry with a little extra ground almonds and turn over onto the worktop. Peel off the paper. Cut out circles and ease into the wells of the bun tray, re-rolling the offcuts as before to make 12.

Bake in a pre-heated oven without any filling for 6 minutes. Carefully brush with beaten egg.

Place 1 tsp jam in each tart. Roll out the remaining pastry into an oblong, brush with beaten egg, then cut into strips. Place two strips in a cross on top of the jam, egg-side down to stick them together. Brush with egg. Bake for 8–10 minutes until nicely browned. Cool in tray, then carefully loosen with a knife and ease out onto racks and leave until cold.

These are best served on the same day.

170 g ground almonds

20 g icing sugar

60 g unsalted butter – diced

1 egg – beaten

Raspberry or other jam

12-hole non-stick bun tin well greased with melted butter

Oven temperature
180°C/350°F/Gas 4

PECAN MAPLE PIE

PASTRY

170 g ground almonds

20 g icing sugar

60 g unsalted butter

FILLING

80 g unsalted butter

100 g soft brown sugar

100 ml maple syrup

Grated rind of 1 orange

3 eggs – beaten

200 g pecan nuts

20 cm loose-based flan tin, well greased and base-lined

Oven temperature
150°C/300°F/Gas 2

Makes one 20 cm pie.

TO MAKE THE PASTRY CASE: Mix the ground almonds and icing sugar together. Mix in the butter and knead lightly to form a dough.

Place a piece of all-purpose food wrap on the worktop, put the dough on top and cover with a piece of baking parchment or greaseproof paper. Roll out between the food wrap and paper until large enough to line the tin. Remove the top piece of paper. Invert the dough, still on the food wrap, into the tin. Press the dough into the base and up the sides of the tin. Remove the food wrap and neaten and trim the top edge. Prick the base and bake in a pre-heated oven for 12 minutes.

FILLING: Melt the butter, add the sugar, maple syrup and orange rind, and then heat gently to dissolve. Stir in the eggs. Carefully place the pecans, round side up, in the pastry case and spoon the filling over. Bake for about 40 minutes until set.

Allow to stand for 15 minutes to firm up, then carefully slide the flan ring off, leaving the pie on the base. Serve warm or cold with ice cream or cream.

LEMON TART

The pastry of this tart loses its crispness when baked, but is still delicious to eat. Makes one 20 cm tart.

Mix the sugar with the eggs and the extra yolk, stirring until smooth. Stir in the cream. Add the rind – use the rind of two lemons if you prefer a tangier filling – and then add the lemon juice, mixing until smooth.

Pour the filling into the pastry case and place in the oven. Take great care as you do this as the case is quite full. If any filling gets between the pastry and the tin it will set and make the tart difficult to remove.

Bake in a pre-heated oven for about 30 minutes until the filling is just set. Leave to cool for a few minutes and then glaze if you wish by sprinkling with caster sugar and caramelising the sugar with a cook's blow torch. If you prefer, simply sprinkle a little sifted icing sugar over the top of the tart and leave to cool.

When cold remove the outer flan ring, leaving the tin base in place. Serve in wedges with a little cream.

One freshly baked sweet flan case, in the flan tin (see recipe on page 150)

170 g caster sugar

3 whole eggs plus 1 extra yolk

130 ml double cream

Rind of 1–2 lemons

4 tblsp lemon juice – about 2 lemons

Caster sugar or icing sugar to finish

Oven temperature 150°C/300°F/Gas 2

CONTINENTAL CHEESECAKE

PASTRY

15 g icing sugar

145 g ground almonds

50 g unsalted butter

FILLING

80 g caster sugar

60 g unsalted butter

250 g ricotta cheese

150 g cream cheese

3 eggs – lightly beaten

45 ml double cream

Grated rind and juice of
1 lemon

25 g ground almonds

30 g raisins

Icing sugar to finish

*One 23 cm loose-based
sandwich pan, greased and
base-lined with baking
parchment*

*Oven temperature
170°C/325°F/Gas 3*

Makes one 23 cm cheesecake to serve 10–12.

TO MAKE THE PASTRY: Mix icing sugar with ground almonds. Rub in butter until the mix resembles breadcrumbs and then knead lightly to make a dough and roll it into a ball. Spread a piece of all-purpose food wrap on the worktop and put the ball of dough on top. Cover with a piece of baking parchment or greaseproof paper.

Roll out to a circle large enough to line the tin. Peel off the top layer of paper and upturn the dough into the prepared tin, still on the food wrap. Fit the dough into the base and up the sides and then peel off the food wrap. Neaten the pastry edges and prick the base. Bake without filling in a pre-heated oven for 10 minutes until lightly browned and firm.

Reduce oven temperature to 150°C/300°F/Gas 2.

TO MAKE THE FILLING: Beat sugar and butter until smooth and light. Beat in the cheeses and then add the eggs and cream. Beat well. Stir in the lemon rind and juice, the almonds and the raisins. Pour into the pastry case. Bake for 35–40 minutes until set in the centre.

As soon as it's removed from the oven, run a thin-bladed knife between the pastry and the tin. Leave to cool in the tin.

Remove the outer ring, leaving the cheesecake on the base and place on a serving dish.

Dust with a little icing sugar. Serve slightly warm or chilled, with cream or fruit compôte.

MINCE PIES

170 g ground almonds

20 g icing sugar

60 g unsalted butter – diced

Mincemeat – (see recipe on page 152)

1 egg – beaten

Caster sugar to finish

Non-stick bun tray, well greased with butter

Oven temperature 170°C/325°F/Gas 3

Makes 7–8 small pies.

Mix the ground almonds and icing sugar in a bowl. Add the butter and rub in until the mixture resembles breadcrumbs. Knead lightly until it holds together.

Place a piece of greaseproof paper on the worktop, place the pastry on top and cover with a piece of all-purpose food wrap or another piece of greaseproof paper. Roll out between the papers to a little over ½ cm thick and peel off the top paper. Lightly dust the surface of the pastry with a little extra sifted ground almonds and turn over onto the worktop. Peel off the paper.

Cut out circles of dough to fit the wells of the bun tray and ease into place. Bake in a pre-heated oven for 3 minutes. (Chill remainder of pastry while the bases bake.) Put a teaspoon of mincemeat into each well, taking care not to damage the pastry.

Roll out the remaining pastry as before and cut smaller circles to fit the top. Brush the edges of the lids with a little beaten egg and turn egg side down onto the mincemeat. Gently press to seal the edges. Brush tops with beaten egg, sprinkle with caster sugar and cut two or three slits in the lids with a very sharp knife.

Bake for about 15 minutes until golden brown. Leave in the tray to cool. When cold, very carefully twist each pie to loosen and then, very gently, ease out of the tin using a plastic knife.

LEMON MERINGUE PIES

Makes 12.

Mix the ground almonds and icing sugar in a bowl. Rub in the butter until the mix is like breadcrumbs, then knead lightly until the mix holds together. Form into a ball.

Spread a piece of all-purpose food wrap on the worktop, place the pastry on top and cover with a piece of greaseproof paper. Roll out to required thickness. Peel off the top paper and sprinkle lightly with a little extra ground almonds. Turn the pastry over onto the worktop and peel off the food wrap.

Cut out circles of pastry and fit into the wells of the prepared bun tray. Re-roll the pastry as before until all the wells are lined. Bake in a pre-heated oven for about 15 minutes until cooked and lightly browned. If the bases puff up during cooking gently press them down with the back of a spoon. Leave in the tins until just cool.

TO MAKE THE FILLING: Whip the cream and then stir in the milk and lemon rind. Add 2 tblsp of lemon juice, stirring well until the mix thickens. Add a little more lemon juice if necessary to thicken the mix.

Place a teaspoon of filling in each case and smooth the top. Very carefully ease the pies out of the bun tray, using a plastic blade to help, and place on a grill pan rack.

TO MAKE THE TOPPING: Whisk the egg whites until stiff and then whisk in the sugar, a spoonful at a time. Spoon into a piping bag fitted with a large plain nozzle. Pipe meringue over the top of each pie, covering the filling completely. Sprinkle a little caster sugar over the tops.

Place under a grill, pre-heated to low, until browned and crispy. Serve soon after making as they soften over time.

PASTRY

150 g ground almonds

20 g icing sugar

50 g unsalted butter

FILLING

60 ml double cream

100 g condensed milk

Grated rind of 2–3 lemons

2–4 tblsp lemon juice

TOPPING

2 egg whites

90 g caster sugar + a little extra for sprinkling

Non-stick bun trays, well greased

Oven temperature 150°C/300°F/Gas 2

APPLE PARCELS

PANCAKE PASTRY

2 eggs

80 ml cold water

30 g ground almonds

A little oil to grease

FILLING

1 Golden Delicious eating apple or other floury eating apple – peeled and grated

20 g raisins

20 g currants

1 tblsp ground almonds plus a little extra for sprinkling

25 g unsalted butter – melted

Caster sugar to sprinkle

Icing sugar to finish

Non-stick baking tray

Oven temperature
180°C/350°F/Gas 4

These are a cross between apple pies and apple strudel and very easy to make. Makes 4 individual parcels. (Also see photograph on page 92.)

TO MAKE THE PANCAKE PASTRY: Mix the eggs with the water in a jug until well blended. Add the ground almonds and mix together well using a wire whisk. Do not use an electric mixer or blender. Put one tablespoon of the mix in a cup, add a little extra ground almonds and mix to a paste. Set aside.

Heat a non-stick frying pan, grease lightly and pour in a quarter of the batter, swirling to make a largish pancake. Cook until lightly browned on the underside and the top is just set. Turn the pancake and cook for 2–3 seconds on the second side. Remove and stack on a plate while you make the remaining pancakes.

FILLING: Mix the grated apple with the raisins, currants and 1 tblsp of ground almonds. Lay the pancakes out on the worktop, browned side up. Brush generously with melted butter and sprinkle with a little extra ground almonds.

Place a quarter of the apple mix in the centre of each one, shaping it to a square cushion. Fold the sides of the pancake up and onto the top of the apple. Spread a little of the almond paste on the top and bottom edges and draw them over the apple to just meet in the centre. Carefully turn the parcels over, and place on the baking tray.

Generously brush melted butter over the sides and tops and sprinkle liberally with caster sugar. Bake in a pre-heated oven for 10 minutes. Brush again with melted butter and sprinkle again with caster sugar and bake for another 10–15 minutes until nicely browned.

Dust with icing sugar and serve warm with cream or ice cream.

 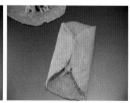 

RASPBERRY & STRAWBERRY SPONGE FLAN

FLAN

90 g icing sugar

155 g ground almonds

3 eggs – separated, plus
1 extra white

½ tsp vanilla essence

FILLING

400–500 g raspberries and
strawberries, washed and
dried if necessary.

8 tblsp redcurrant jelly

1 tsp lemon juice

1 tsp water

*27 cm diameter sponge flan
tin, preferably non-stick, well
buttered and centre-lined*

*Oven temperature
170°C/325°F/Gas 3*

Makes one 27 cm sponge flan to serve 8–10.

Sift icing sugar and ground almonds together twice. Beat yolks with essence in a small jug.

Whisk egg whites until very stiff. Pour yolk mix over whites and mix together thoroughly using a wire whisk. Sprinkle almond mix on top and use a metal spoon to mix together carefully and lightly.

Spoon into the prepared tin, making sure there are no air pockets in the rim. Smooth the surface and bake in a pre-heated oven for about 25 minutes until evenly browned and firm. Cool in tin for 10 minutes and then ease the sides away from the tin. Turn out onto a serving plate and leave to cool completely.

FILLING: Arrange the fruit in rings in the flan, starting at the outside. Warm the redcurrant jelly with the lemon juice and water, stirring until the jelly melts. Cool a little until almost on the point of setting and then spoon over the fruit, filling any gaps between the fruit. Use a pastry brush to brush jelly over the fruit in a thin film, warm the jelly slightly if it is setting too quickly, and leave to set.

Serve with whipped cream, preferably within 3 hours of assembling. It is just as delicious after this but the juices from the fruit start to seep into the sponge.

BAKED SYRUP SPONGES

These are gorgeous – they miss none of the syrupy texture and taste of a steamed pud! Serve with extra syrup, pouring cream or real vanilla custard for a perfect winter pudding, or comfort food anytime.
Makes 5 individual sponges.

Put one level dstsp of golden syrup in the base of each cup.

Sift the ground almonds and icing sugar together twice. Beat the egg yolks with the vanilla essence.

Beat the egg whites until very stiff. Pour the yolks over the whites and mix together thoroughly using a wire whisk. Sprinkle the almond mix over the top and fold in using a large metal spoon. Spoon the mixture on top of the syrup in the cups. Don't overfill as the mix rises up and then sinks back as it cooks.

Bake in a pre-heated oven for about 25 minutes until the centres are just firm. Remove from the oven, run a knife around the edges to loosen, and turn out onto serving plates. Serve at once.

5 dstsp golden syrup

120 g ground almonds

80 g icing sugar

3 eggs – separated

½ tsp vanilla essence

5 ovenproof cups – about 200 ml size – well buttered

Oven temperature 170°C/325°F/Gas 3

OLD-FASHIONED SHERRY TRIFLE

8 sponge fingers (see pages 40 and 57) OR about 50 g cake offcuts, such as Swiss roll trimmings (see pages 38 and 46)

Raspberry jam

24 raspberries – about 80 g

4 flour-free amaretti biscuits OR 12 small ratafia biscuits

100 ml sweet sherry

Grated rind of ½ lemon

16 blanched almonds – chopped

VANILLA CUSTARD

200 ml full-cream milk

50 ml double cream

2 whole eggs plus 2 yolks

40 g caster sugar

Few drops vanilla essence

TO FINISH

125 ml double cream

A few flaked almonds, plain or toasted

4 pretty glasses

For a non-alcoholic version replace the sherry with orange juice. If raspberries are not available just use the raspberry jam. Serves 4.

Spread the sponge fingers or cake trimmings with jam and cut into pieces. Place in the base of the glasses, putting the raspberries in the gaps. Crush the amaretti or ratafia biscuits and sprinkle over. Pour the sherry over the top. Sprinkle the lemon rind and chopped almonds on top.

TO MAKE THE CUSTARD USING A DOUBLE BOILER: Heat the milk and cream in a small saucepan to almost boiling. Mix the eggs with the extra yolks and sugar together in a largish jug. Stirring briskly, pour on the hot milk. Strain into the top of a double saucepan. Put hot water in the lower pan, making sure it doesn't touch the base of the top pan. Maintaining the water at a simmer stir the custard constantly with a wooden spoon until it thickens – this may take 10 or more minutes. When the custard is thick enough to coat the back of the wooden spoon remove the pan from the heat and stir in the essence. Strain into a clean jug and allow to cool for a few minutes. Pour over the amaretti, leave to cool and then put in the fridge until cold.

Whip the cream until it just holds its shape and spoon onto the custard in small dots. Using two forks, carefully spread the cream in an even layer. Sprinkle with flaked almonds and chill.

NOTE: Do not allow the water in the double saucepan to boil or the custard may curdle. This custard may be made in a heavy based pan over a very gentle heat if you do not have a double boiler. Follow the method for vanilla custard on page 153.

PINEAPPLE UPSIDE DOWN

50 g unsalted butter

100 g muscovado sugar

4 rings tinned pineapple

SPONGE LAYER

110 g ground almonds

80 g icing sugar

3 eggs – separated

*16 cm square solid-base
cake tin, greased*

*Oven temperature
170°C/325°F/Gas 3*

Makes one pudding to serve 4–6.

Melt the butter and stir in the sugar until well mixed. Spread in the base of the prepared cake tin. Drain the pineapple rings and arrange them on top of the sugar mix.

Sift the ground almonds and the icing sugar twice, making sure that they are well mixed.

Beat the egg yolks with a fork.

Whisk the egg whites until very stiff. Pour the yolks over the whites and mix thoroughly using a wire whisk. Sprinkle the almond mix over the top and stir in using a large metal spoon. Spoon over the top of the pineapple and smooth the top.

Bake in a pre-heated oven for about 30–35 minutes until cooked and firm to the touch.

Place a serving plate on top of the tin and carefully turn over. Lift off the baking tin. Serve at once with custard or pouring cream.

STRAWBERRY & APPLE CRUMBLE

Serves 4.

Core the apples and chop into small pieces. Slice the strawberries into thick slices and mix with the apple. Add 1–2 tblsp sugar to taste. Put into the prepared dish and bake in a pre-heated oven for 10 minutes.

Mix the ground almonds and sugar. Rub in the butter until the mix resembles breadcrumbs. Stir in the hazelnuts. Sprinkle the topping over the fruit and bake for about 20 minutes or until nicely browned. Serve with cream, ice cream or vanilla custard.

2 medium sized floury eating apples

450 g strawberries – wiped clean

1–2 tblsp sugar

75 g ground almonds

50 g sugar

50 g soft unsalted butter

50 g chopped roasted hazelnuts

A deep oven-proof dish, buttered

Oven temperature 170°C/325°F/Gas 3

STRAWBERRY SHORTCAKE

SHORTCAKE

350 g ground almonds

50 g icing sugar

120 g unsalted butter

FILLING AND TOPPING

400 g strawberries

450 ml double cream

½ tsp vanilla essence

2 tblsp sifted icing sugar

*Three baking sheets lined
with baking parchment*

*Oven temperature
150°C/300°F/Gas 2*

*This makes a very rich finish to a summer lunch or dinner. Don't be put
off by the length of the instructions – it is very easy to make. Makes 8
generous portions.*

Sift the ground almonds with the icing sugar. Rub in the butter and then
knead lightly to a dough. Divide the dough into three and roll into balls.

Spread a piece of all-purpose food wrap on the worktop, place a ball of
dough on top and cover with a piece of baking parchment or greaseproof
paper. Roll out to a 20 cm circle. Peel off and reserve the paper. Carefully
lift the dough on the food wrap and invert onto a prepared baking sheet.
Peel off the food wrap and neaten the edges of the dough. Repeat with the
remaining dough balls.

Bake in a pre-heated oven for about 16–18 minutes until lightly browned,
swapping the trays if necessary to ensure even browning. As soon as they
are cooked select the best one as the top. Using a sharp knife cut the top
into quarters, then cut each quarter into two. Leave on the baking trays until
completely cold.

FILLING AND TOPPING: Reserve 9 of the biggest and best strawberries,
leaving the hulls in place, then hull and slice the rest.

Whip the cream until stiff. Mix in the essence and the icing sugar. Put just
under a quarter of the cream into a forcing bag fitted with a large star food
nozzle. Fold the sliced strawberries into the remaining cream.

Place a shortcake round on a serving plate, put half the strawberry mix on
top and spread evenly, taking care as the shortbread is fragile. Place a
second disc on top and spread with remaining strawberry mixture.

Pipe 8 rosettes, evenly spaced, around the edge of the cake. Place a
strawberry on top of each rosette, pointing to the centre. Place the shortcake
triangles around the cake, points meeting in the centre, and each one
leaning on a strawberry. Pipe one more rosette in the centre and place the
last strawberry on top.

NOTE: This will soften with keeping and is best served within two hours of
assembly. It is just as delicious after this but not as crisp.

BLUEBERRY CHEESECAKES

4 tblsp blueberry jam with plenty of fruit

150 g full-fat soft cheese (see notes)

6 level tblsp yoghurt

50 g caster sugar

Finely grated rind of 1 lemon

1½ tsp gelatine

2 tblsp very hot water

20 g unsalted butter

4 grain-free amaretti biscuits or home-made almond or hazelnut biscuits

TO FINISH

Fresh blueberries

Whipped cream

Fresh mint

4 ramekins base-lined with a circle of baking parchment

Makes 4.

Divide the jam between the ramekins.

Mix the cheese and yoghurt together. Add the sugar and beat until smooth then beat in lemon rind.

Sprinkle the gelatine over the hot water and stir until dissolved. Beating all the time pour the gelatine into the cheese mixture. Divide between the ramekins, leaving a ½ cm space at the top of the dishes. Chill for an hour or two until set.

Melt the butter. Crush the amaretti or biscuits finely then stir into the melted butter. Divide the mix into four portions. Working on a piece of greaseproof paper or baking parchment pat a portion of the biscuit mix into a neat round. Place on top of the cheese mix. Repeat with the remaining mixture. Chill well.

Just before serving run a thin-bladed knife around the cheesecakes and turn out onto serving plates. Peel off paper. Decorate with fresh blueberries and a swirl of cream topped with a mint sprig.

VARIATION. Omit the jam and pile fresh raspberries or sliced strawberries on top. Serve with raspberry or strawberry coulis.

CHEESE BLINTZES

Makes about 10.

TO MAKE THE PANCAKES: Mix the eggs and the water in a jug and add the ground almonds, mixing well with a wire whisk. Do not use an electric mixer or blender.

Heat a non-stick frying pan and lightly oil. There should be no need to oil after making the first one. Pour a little batter into the pan and swirl to make a nice even pancake about 18 cm in diameter. Cook until nicely browned on the underside and the top is set.

Turn the pancake using a spatula and cook for 2–3 seconds only on the other side. Pile onto a plate with the cooked side uppermost. Continue until all the mixture is used, stirring well before each pouring.

FOR THE FILLING: Mix the ricotta cheese, caster sugar, drained raisins and lemon rind. Spread the pancakes, cooked side up, on the worktop and put a small spoonful of the cheese mixture in the centre of each one. Fold up the lower edge, then fold in the two sides and the top to make a neat parcel.

TO FINISH: Roll each parcel in the icing sugar. Melt the butter in the frying pan and fry the blintzes until browned on all sides. Keep warm until they are all cooked and serve at once with sour cream, fromage frais, or fruit.

VARIATION: If you can eat cinnamon then add ½ tsp to the icing sugar for rolling the parcels before frying.

BATTER

3 eggs

120 ml cold water

45 g ground almonds

A little oil

FILLING

250 g ricotta cheese

1–2 tblsp caster sugar to taste

25 g raisins, plumped in hot water

Grated rind of 1 lemon

TO FINISH

3 tblsp icing sugar

25 g unsalted butter for frying

CHRISTMAS
PUDDING

150 g currants

150 g sultanas

150 g raisins

75 g semi-dried figs

75 g candied peel

(see recipe on page 156)

75 g blanched almonds

75 g dried cherries

Juice and rind of 1 lemon

6 tblsp rum

6 tblsp port

2 tblsp liquid honey

100 g soft brown sugar

200 g ground almonds

3 eggs – separated

*Glass or china pudding
basins, or oven-proof
cups, of the chosen size,
well-greased*

*Makes 2 x 600 ml puddings. Or 1 x 600 ml pudding and 6 x 100 ml
individual puddings.*

Mix the currants, sultanas and raisins in a large glass or china bowl. Chop
the figs, peel and almonds and add to the currant mix. Then add the
cherries and lemon rind. Mix the lemon juice, rum, port and honey and
pour over the fruit, stirring well. Leave for several hours, stirring occasionally,
until the fruit has plumped and absorbed the liquid.

Sift the sugar and ground almonds together. Whisk the egg whites until very
stiff. Beat the yolks together and pour over the whites, mixing together well
with a wire whisk. Tip the fruit on top and stir in. Add the almond mix and
stir all together using a large metal spoon.

Spoon into the prepared basins and smooth the tops. Cover the basins with
well-buttered greaseproof paper and then with a double layer of foil. Tie
tightly with string.

Half fill a steamer with boiling water and place the puddings in the top.
Steam the larger puddings for 5 hours and the individual ones for 2 hours,
topping up the steamer with boiling water as required. Allow to cool and
then renew the coverings.

TO REHEAT: Place the puddings in the steamer as before and steam for
2 hours for the larger ones and 1 hour for the individual ones.

Serve with brandy or rum butter, or with cream.

TIRAMISU

Serves 2.

Mix the mascarpone with the cream, icing sugar and vanilla essence.

Dissolve the coffee in the hot water and add the rum if using. Pour into a bowl. Add the amaretti, turning them in the liquid until saturated.

Put one amaretti in the base of each glass, if necessary breaking it apart a little to fit. Spoon over a little of the liquid.

Divide about ¼ of the mascarpone cream between the two glasses, smoothing it level. Sprinkle over ¼ of the grated chocolate.

Place two more amaretti biscuits in each glass, again breaking apart if necessary to make an even layer. Spoon over a little more of the liquid so the biscuit layer is quite moist. Divide the remaining cream between the two glasses. Add the rest of the chocolate.

Refrigerate until required. Best served on day of making.

NOTE: If straight glasses are used then use half of the amaretti and mascarpone for the layers. Strong filtered coffee or expresso may be used in place of the coffee granules and water.

100 g mascarpone

60 ml double cream

1½–2 tblsp icing sugar

¼ tsp vanilla essence

1½ tsp good coffee granules

4 tblsp hot water

2 tsp rum – optional

6 flour-free amaretti biscuits

25 g dark chocolate – grated (see notes)

Two cocktail glasses

PANCAKES & WAFFLES

I love waffles. I love them with maple syrup and fresh fruit, especially raspberries. And then I came up with the recipe for Chocolate Waffles with a simple chocolate sauce so I'm hooked on those too. But I also enjoy pancakes, with loads of freshly squeezed lemon juice and a generous sprinkling of caster sugar. In this chapter I have also included a recipe for Chocolate Pancakes with a very rich chocolate sauce – strictly adults only! And for a special occasion a rich and deliciously satisfying version of Crêpes Suzette. But within other chapters of this book the humble pancake becomes so much more than we are used to. In a slightly thicker guise it forms the layers in the lasagnes. It also makes great salad wraps for a picnic or snack lunch. And in a slightly undercooked form they become the 'pastry' for Samosas and Apple Parcels, crisping up beautifully when baked.

Pancakes? I didn't think you could have those ...

BASIC PANCAKES

2 eggs

80 ml cold water

30 g sifted ground almonds

A little olive oil

Makes about 6 pancakes depending on size.

Mix the eggs with the water in a mixing jug. Add the ground almonds. Stir together using a wire whisk but do not beat. Do not use an electric mixer or a blender.

Heat a non-stick frying pan over a medium heat. Lightly oil the pan. It shouldn't be necessary to add further oil after the first one.

Stir the pancake mix just before pouring each one. Pour a sixth of the batter into the pan, turning the pan to shape a nice even pancake.

Cook until set on the top and browned on the underside. Using a spatula turn the pancake and cook on the second side. If the pancake tears, spoon a little mix into the tear and it will cook and seal. When the second side is cooked turn it back again for a few seconds. Stack on a plate in a warm oven if to be served warm.

NOTE: If using as the pastry for samosas don't overcook the pancakes, as they need to be pliable.

CHOCOLATE PANCAKES
WITH CHOCOLATE SAUCE

Makes 12 pancakes to serve 4–6.

TO MAKE THE PANCAKES: Mix the eggs with the water in a jug. Mix the ground almonds with the cocoa powder and add to the eggs, stirring well with a wire whisk. Do not use an electric mixer or blender.

Heat a non-stick frying pan and lightly oil. Stir the pancake mix and pour a little into the pan, swirling to make a nice even pancake. Cook for a few minutes until the top is set and the base cooked, and then turn and cook the other side. Stirring the mix before each pouring, make the remaining pancakes, keeping them warm in a low oven as they are made.

TO MAKE THE SAUCE: Put the cream, butter and syrup into a pan and heat until the butter is melted. Add the chocolate and vanilla and stir until the chocolate is melted and the sauce is smooth.

Roll the pancakes and serve with the sauce spooned over. May be accompanied by a selection of fresh fruit.

PANCAKES

4 eggs

180 ml cold water

60 g ground almonds

3 tsp cocoa powder

A little olive oil

SAUCE

100 ml double cream

20 g unsalted butter

2 tblsp golden syrup

100 g dark chocolate (see notes) – broken into pieces

½ tsp vanilla essence

These have rather fallen out of favour but they are so easy to make and are quite delicious. The pancakes can be prepared ahead of time and reheated in the sauce when required.

PANCAKES

3 eggs

120 ml cold water

45 g sifted ground almonds

A little olive oil

SAUCE

100 g unsalted butter

75 g caster sugar

Rind and juice of 2 oranges

2–3 tblsp rum

CRÊPES SUZETTE

Makes 8–10 pancakes. Allow 2 pancakes per person.

TO MAKE THE PANCAKES: Mix the eggs and water in a jug using a wire whisk. Add the ground almonds and mix well together. Do not use an electric mixer or blender.

Heat a non-stick frying pan and lightly oil. Stir the batter and pour a good spoonful into the pan, swirling to make a nice even pancake. Cook for a few minutes until lightly browned on the underside and set on top. Turn using a spatula and cook the other side. Stack on a plate while you make the rest, stirring the batter before each pouring.

TO MAKE THE SAUCE: Put all the sauce ingredients in a large frying pan. Heat gently until the butter has melted and the sugar dissolved. Turn up the heat and allow to boil for 2–3 minutes until syrupy.

Taking one pancake at a time, lay it flat in the sauce with the side that was cooked first underneath. Spoon a little sauce over and allow time to heat through, then fold in half using a spatula and spoon. Fold in half again and leave to one side of the pan. Continue with the remaining pancakes.

Serve on warm plates with a little whipped cream to accompany.

SCOTCH PANCAKES

Makes about 6 small pancakes.

Sift the almonds and the baking powder twice. Heat a frying pan over a medium heat.

Mix egg and milk together, add to the almonds and stir briskly to mix. Stir in sultanas.

Lightly oil the heated pan. Drop spoonfuls of the mixture onto the pan and cook until browned underneath and bubbles appear on the surface. Turn and cook the second side, making sure they are cooked right through.

Serve with butter and jam.

55 g ground almonds

½ tsp baking powder – see notes

1 egg

3 tblsp milk

25 g sultanas

A little olive oil

ASPARAGUS CHEESE PANCAKES

250 g fresh asparagus

100 ml double cream

100 g cheese – grated

6 basic pancakes (see recipe on page 120)

Oven-proof dish, well greased

Oven temperature 180°C/350°F/Gas 4

Makes 6.

Snap off the tough ends of the asparagus and steam for about 5 minutes until just tender.

Put the cream and ¾ of the cheese in a small saucepan. Stir over a medium heat until the cheese melts and the sauce has thickened slightly.

Lay out the pancakes and place 2 or 3 asparagus spears in the centre of each one. Spoon over a little sauce, roll the pancake up and place in a single layer in the prepared dish. Pour the remaining sauce over the top and sprinkle the rest of the cheese on top.

Bake in a pre-heated oven for about 20 minutes until golden and bubbling. Serve with salad leaves.

BACON BRUNCH PANCAKES

Makes 4 small pancakes.

Sift the ground almonds, baking powder and salt together. Mix the cream with the egg and 2 tblsp water.

Heat one tablespoon of the oil in a non-stick frying pan over a medium heat. Add the bacon and onion and fry until cooked through and starting to brown.

Cool slightly and then stir into the cream mixture. Add the almonds and stir well. The mix should just have a dropping consistency. If too thick add the extra tablespoon of water.

Heat remaining oil in the pan and drop spoonfuls of the mixture in four flat rounds, smoothing the tops. Cook for 5–6 minutes until nicely browned on the underside. Use a fish slice to turn, then cook for another 5–6 minutes. They should be cooked through and firm when pressed, so if necessary cook a few minutes longer, turning once or twice.

Serve with fried eggs and grilled tomatoes, or simply with butter.

60 g ground almonds

½ tsp baking powder (see notes)

Pinch of salt

1 tblsp double cream

1 egg

2–3 tblsp water

2 tblsp olive oil

4 rashers streaky bacon – chopped

1 small onion – finely chopped

WAFFLES

4 eggs – separated

4 dstsp unsalted butter – melted

120 g ground almonds

A little olive oil

Heat the waffle iron according to the instructions

Makes about 6 waffles depending on the size of the waffle iron. (Also see photograph on page 118.)

Mix the egg yolks with the melted butter. Whisk whites until very stiff. Pour yolk mixture over the whites and mix together thoroughly using a wire whisk. Sprinkle the ground almonds over the top and stir until just mixed.

Lightly oil the waffle iron and put a good spoonful of the mix in the centre. Lower the lid and hold it firmly in place for a few seconds to allow the batter to spread. Cook for a few minutes until browned and cooked. Remove the waffle and keep warm while you cook the remaining mixture.

If you prefer crisper waffles, put them under a pre-heated grill for a few seconds each side before serving.

Serve with maple syrup, butter, honey or fruit.

CHOCOLATE WAFFLES &
SIMPLE CHOCOLATE SAUCE

Makes 4–6 waffles depending on the size of the waffle iron.

Mix the egg yolks with the melted butter. Mix the ground almonds with the cocoa powder and the icing sugar and sift together.

Whisk the egg whites until very stiff, pour the yolk mixture over the top and mix well using a wire whisk. Sprinkle the almond mix on top and stir together using a wire whisk.

Lightly oil the waffle iron. Place a spoonful of the batter in the centre of the iron and hold the lid shut to allow the batter to spread evenly. Cook until the waffle is firm right through. Keep in a warm oven while you make the rest.

TO MAKE THE SAUCE: Put all the ingredients except the cream in a saucepan over a gentle heat. Stir until the butter has melted and the sugar dissolved. Continue stirring for 1–2 minutes until the sauce is smooth. Add the cream and stir well.

If you prefer crisper waffles, put them under a pre-heated grill for a few seconds each side before serving. Serve the waffles on warm plates with the sauce spooned over.

WAFFLES

3 eggs – separated

3 tblsp melted butter

90 g ground almonds

2 tblsp cocoa powder

2 tblsp icing sugar

A little olive oil

SAUCE

100 g unsalted butter

50 g light brown muscovado sugar

2 tblsp golden syrup

2 dstsp cocoa powder

2–3 tblsp double cream

Heat the waffle iron according to the instructions

FLANS & SAVOURIES

Why is it that as soon as you can't have something you realise how much you want it? I never realised until I couldn't eat any grain at all just how much I enjoyed the occasional samosa. So it was a big challenge to make a samosa that equalled – at least to me – those I had to forego. They may seem a bit fiddly compared to the other recipes but they are well worth the little extra trouble. And as they don't contain any spices they don't upset me at all. I also missed pizza, now part of most people's lives, so I've included a Picnic Pizza, which has all the taste and is perfect for travelling, or just eating as a snack in the hand. There are several quiches and flans – perfect when served with a big green salad for meals anytime. They're all easy to make and include a variety of fillings so there's something for everyone. Also, because one of the things off the menu is pasta, I've included a couple of lasagnes, one meat and one vegetarian. Both are easy to make and rich and satisfying. However, if it's a crispy nibble with a pre-dinner drink that you miss try the Sesame Cheese Biscuits – I guarantee you won't be able to stop at one!

I must have been hungrier than I thought ...

FRENCH ONION TART

One freshly baked cheese
flan case, in the flan tin
(see recipe on page 151)

50 g butter

700 g onions

2 eggs

120 ml double cream

½ tsp salt or to taste

Oven temperature
170°C/325°F/Gas 3

Makes one 23 cm tart.

Melt the butter in a large frying pan. Slice the onions thinly and add to the pan. Stir well, cover the pan and cook over a gentle heat for 30–40 minutes, stirring occasionally, until softened and starting to brown. Remove from the heat, allow to cool a little, then tip into a large bowl.

Beat the eggs and mix with the cream and seasoning. Add to the onions and mix thoroughly. Turn into the pastry case. Bake in a pre-heated oven for about 30 minutes until set and lightly browned.

Cool for 5 minutes in the tin, then place on an upturned bowl and carefully slide the outer ring down. Leave on the tin base and serve warm or cold with salads.

ASPARAGUS & SMOKED TROUT FLAN

Makes one 23 cm flan.

Wash the asparagus, snap off the tough ends and steam for 3 minutes. Cool, then cut the stems into three pieces. Roughly flake the trout and place in the base of the pastry case. Lay the asparagus over the top.

Beat the eggs with the cream cheese and salt. When well blended stir in the cream and lemon rind. Pour over the asparagus. Sprinkle on the cheese.

Bake in a pre-heated oven for about 30 minutes until cooked and lightly browned.

Allow to stand for 5 minutes, then place on an upturned bowl and slide the outer ring down. Leave on the tin base and serve warm or cold.

One freshly baked cheese flan case, in the flan tin (see recipe on page 151)

200–250 g asparagus

125 g smoked trout fillet

3 eggs

75 g cream cheese

Good pinch of salt

50 ml double cream

Grated rind of 1 lemon

3 tblsp finely grated pecorino cheese

Oven temperature
170°C/325°F/Gas 3

CHEESE & BACON QUICHES

PASTRY

100 g ground almonds

40 g unsalted butter – diced

40 g finely grated cheddar-type cheese

FILLING

75 g bacon lardons

50 g grated cheddar-type cheese

2 eggs – beaten

75 ml double cream

Salt to taste

4 x 9 cm loose-based individual flan tins, greased with melted butter and base-lined

Oven temperature 170°C/325°F/Gas 3

Makes 4 x 9 cm quiches.

TO MAKE THE PASTRY: Put the ground almonds into a bowl, add the butter and rub in thoroughly. Stir in the cheese and then knead lightly to form a dough.

Divide into four. Spread a piece of all-purpose food wrap on the work surface, place a ball of dough on top and cover with a piece of baking parchment. Roll out between the food wrap and paper to a circle just large enough to line a tin.

Peel off the top piece of paper and upturn the dough, still on the food wrap, into the tin. Ease the dough into the tin and up the sides, gently pressing it into place. Peel off the food wrap, neaten the dough and trim the top edge. Complete the others.

Bake in a pre-heated oven for about 10 minutes until lightly coloured.

TO MAKE THE FILLING: Put the lardons in a bowl and pour boiling water over them. Leave for 2 minutes, then drain. Divide between the quiches taking care not to damage the pastry. Sprinkle over 30 g of grated cheese. Beat the eggs and cream and season to taste. Pour over the filling. Sprinkle with the remaining cheese.

Return to the oven and bake for 20–25 minutes until lightly browned and puffed up.

Allow to stand for 5 minutes before gently easing the outer flan rings off. Transfer the quiches to serving plates by sliding a fish slice under the pastry and lifting off the base. Serve warm or cold.

CHEESE TARTLETS

PASTRY

50 g butter – diced

140 g ground almonds

50 g finely grated cheddar-type cheese

FILLING

6 tblsp double cream

1 egg

1 tsp wholegrain mustard

75 g finely grated gruyere cheese

Non-stick bun tray, well greased

Oven temperature 150°C/300°F/Gas 2

TO MAKE THE PASTRY: Rub the butter into the ground almonds until the mixture resembles fine breadcrumbs. Stir in the cheese and knead lightly to make a dough.

Spread a piece of greaseproof paper or baking parchment on the worktop. Place the dough in the centre and cover with a sheet of all-purpose food wrap. Roll out fairly thinly between the papers and then peel off the food wrap. Sprinkle a little extra ground almonds over the pastry and then turn over onto the worktop. Remove paper.

Cut out circles of dough and line the wells of the prepared bun tray, re-rolling the pastry as before to make 12 cases. Bake in a pre-heated oven for about 10 minutes until lightly cooked.

TO MAKE THE FILLING: Mix the cream, egg and mustard in a bowl. Stir in the cheese.

Increase the oven temperature to 170°C/325°F/Gas 3.

Spoon the filling into the part-baked cases, stirring the mix between each spoonful. Return the tartlets to the oven and bake for about 12 minutes, or until the filling is risen and set and the pastry browned.

Leave the tartlets in the tray until barely warm then very carefully ease out using a plastic knife. Serve at once or leave until cold.

SPINACH & MUSHROOM FLAN

Makes one 23 cm flan.

Cook spinach as directed on packet, drain and squeeze dry. An easy way to do this is to place it on a plate and cover with another plate as if stacking them. Hold vertically and squeeze over the sink.

Heat the oil in a frying pan over a medium heat. Add the onion and cook until softened but not coloured. Add the mushrooms and cook for a few minutes longer, stirring occasionally. Cool a little.

Beat the eggs, cream, salt and herbs in a large bowl. Stir in the spinach and mix well. Drain the onions and mushrooms, discarding the cooking liquid, and stir into the egg mixture. Pour into the pastry case and sprinkle the cheese over the top.

Bake in a pre-heated oven for 30–35 minutes until set and lightly browned.

Leave to cool for 5 minutes, then place on an upturned bowl and slide the outer ring down. Leave on the tin base and serve warm or cold.

1 freshly baked cheese flan case, in the flan tin (see recipe on page 151)

250 g frozen leaf spinach

2 tblsp oil

1 onion – chopped

150 g button mushrooms – sliced

3 eggs

100 ml double cream

¼–½ tsp salt

Pinch of dried mixed herbs

50 g grated mild cheese

Oven temperature
170°C/325°F/Gas 3

BACON & LEEK FLAN

One freshly baked cheese flan case, in the flan tin (see recipe on page 151)

100 g bacon lardons

1½ tblsp olive oil

500 g leeks – washed and thinly sliced

3 eggs

100 ml double cream

Large pinch salt

1 tsp dried thyme or mixed herbs

1 clove garlic – crushed

3 tblsp finely grated pecorino cheese

Oven temperature
170°C/325°F/Gas 3

Makes one 23 cm flan.

Cover the bacon with boiling water, leave for 2 minutes and then drain. Heat the oil in a large frying pan, add the leeks and cook them gently for about 10 minutes until softened. Cool a little, then mix with the bacon in a large bowl.

Beat the eggs with the cream, salt, herbs and garlic. Pour over the leeks and mix together well. Spoon into the pastry case.

Sprinkle the cheese over the top and bake in a pre-heated oven for about 30 minutes until set and lightly browned.

Allow to stand for 5 minutes, then place on an upturned bowl and slide the outer ring down. Leave on the tin base and serve warm or cold.

LIGHT CHEESE PUDDING

This is almost a soufflé – just not quite as light. However, it is so good that it comes a close second. Serves 3–4 depending on accompaniments and appetite. (Also see photograph on page 128.)

Generously brush the dish with melted butter and sprinkle with the pecorino cheese, turning the dish to coat evenly. Tap out any excess cheese.

Melt the butter in a pan and stir in the ground almonds. Cook over a gentle heat for 1–2 minutes. Pour in the boiling milk and stir briskly with a wire whisk until blended. Add seasoning. Return to heat and bring to the boil. Cook for 2–3 minutes, stirring constantly.

Remove from the heat and add egg yolks, one at a time, mixing well. Return the pan to a gentle heat and stir until the sauce thickens slightly. Take care not to overheat the sauce or it may curdle. Remove from the heat and add all but one tablespoon of the cheese and stir until smooth. Cover the pan and set aside.

Whisk the egg whites until they are very stiff. Fold ¼ of the egg whites into the cheese mixture to lighten, then carefully fold in the remainder using a wire whisk or a large metal spoon.

Pour into the prepared dish, filling almost to the top, and sprinkle with the remaining cheese. Put into the oven, immediately turning the temperature down to 200°C/400°F/Gas 6 and bake for about 30 minutes until nicely browned and set.

Serve at once, with salads. If necessary it can wait for up to 5 minutes in a turned-off oven with the door ajar. Like a soufflé, this will sink as it cools.

A little melted butter

1 tblsp finely grated pecorino cheese

55 g butter

50 g finely ground almonds – weighed after sifting twice

260 ml boiling milk

½ tsp salt

4 egg yolks

85 g finely grated cheddar cheese – or a mixture of cheddar and pecorino

5 egg whites

1 ¼ litre soufflé dish

Oven temperature 220°C/425°F/Gas 7

BAKED CHICKEN NUGGETS

120 g ground almonds

½ tsp salt

1½ tsp dried mixed herbs

250 g pot of low-fat fromage frais or low-fat yoghurt – check it is starch free

400 g skinless and boneless chicken thighs

Two baking trays lined with baking parchment

Oven temperature 190°C/375°F/Gas 5

Makes about 35 pieces.

Mix the ground almonds with the salt and herbs. Put into a shallow bowl.

Put the fromage frais or yoghurt into another shallow bowl.

Cut the chicken into bite-sized pieces. Dip each chicken piece into the fromage frais, then into the almond mix, turning to coat evenly. Place, well spaced apart, on the prepared trays.

Bake in a pre-heated oven for 10–15 minutes. Then turn each piece over – the underside will be quite moist – and bake for a further 10–15 minutes until golden brown and crispy.

Serve warm or cold with salad or as a snack.

NOTE: This can be made using chicken breasts, but the nuggets will then be rather dry.

CHICKEN DIPPERS

4 chicken breasts

12 tblsp ground almonds

12 tblsp very finely grated pecorino cheese

1 egg – well beaten

4 tblsp olive oil

Makes 24.

Cut each chicken breast into six strips.

Mix the ground almonds and cheese in a bowl.

Put the egg into a bowl.

Dip the chicken into the egg, then roll in the ground almond and cheese mixture to evenly coat the pieces. Put on a plate as each one is done.

Heat the oil in a frying pan. Cook the chicken for 5–6 minutes each side, turning frequently, until browned and cooked right through. No pink should remain in the middle and any juice must be clear.

Serve warm or cold with dips or grain-free and starch-free ketchup. Or with salad as a light meal.

FISH FINGERS

80 g ground almonds

¼ tsp salt or to taste

1 egg – beaten

400 g cod or other firm fish
in one or two pieces

A little oil to fry

Makes 20–24 medium-sized fingers.

Sift the ground almonds and salt together, discarding any nut pieces left in the sieve. Put into a shallow bowl.

Put the egg into another shallow bowl.

Cut the fish into even-sized sticks.

Dip each piece of fish into the beaten egg and then into the almond mixture to lightly coat each one.

Heat the oil in a frying pan and fry the fingers for about 10–12 minutes, turning several times until evenly browned and thoroughly cooked.

Serve at once.

NOTE: If your diet allows, ¼–½ tsp turmeric, sifted with the ground almonds, will give the familiar colour to the fish fingers.

PICNIC PIZZA

Makes about 8 pieces.

Whisk the egg whites until very stiff.

Mix the egg yolks with a fork and pour over the whites. Mix well together using a wire whisk. Sprinkle the ground almonds over the top of the egg mix and fold in using a large metal spoon. Turn into the prepared tin and smooth the top.

Sprinkle the cheese evenly over the pizza base. Cut the tomatoes into strips. Cut the anchovies into strips lengthways. Cut the olives into three or four rings. Arrange all on top of the cheese. Sprinkle the herbs over the top.

Bake in a pre-heated oven for 18–20 minutes until browned and crispy looking. Turn out and eat warm or cold.

3 eggs – separated

85 g ground almonds

75 g finely grated pecorino cheese

6 halves sun-dried tomato (in oil)

8 anchovy fillets

12 pitted green olives

1 tsp dried mixed herbs

Non-stick baking tin, 32 x 22 cm, oiled

Oven temperature 180°C/350°F/Gas 4

SPINACH & CHEESE LASAGNE

60 g butter

500 g frozen spinach, cooked, squeezed dry and chopped

Salt to taste

250 g ricotta cheese

About 10 lasagne pancakes (see recipe on page 155)

About 500 ml double cream

170 g grated cheddar-type cheese

25 x 16 cm lasagne dish

Oven temperature 180°C/350°F/Gas 4

Serves 6–8 depending on appetite.

Melt the butter in a pan and toss the spinach in it for 2–3 minutes. Cool slightly and mix with the seasoning and ricotta cheese.

Spread a thin layer of the spinach mixture in the base of the dish. Cover with a layer of pancakes. Divide the remaining spinach mixture into four portions. Place one portion over the pancakes. Pour over ¼ of the cream, then ¼ of the grated cheese.

Repeat the pancake, spinach, cream and cheese layers, finishing with a cheese layer.

Bake in a pre-heated oven for 30–40 minutes until nicely browned and really hot right through. Allow to stand in a warm place for 10 minutes before serving with salads.

MEAT LASAGNE

Serves 6–8 depending on appetite.

Spread a thin layer of meat sauce in the base of the dish. Cover with a layer of pancakes, trimmed to fit if necessary.

Spread ¼ of the remaining meat sauce on top of the pancakes. Evenly pour ¼ of the cream over the meat sauce then sprinkle with ¼ of the cheese. Repeat the pancake, meat sauce, cream and cheese layers until you have four layers of pancakes in total, finishing with a cheese layer.

TOPPING: Add the 20 g of cheese to the top layer, and sprinkle with the oregano if using.

Bake in a pre-heated oven for about 40 minutes or until heated right through and well browned and bubbling. Keep warm for 10–15 minutes to allow lasagne to rest and firm a little. Serve with salad.

1 x meat sauce (see recipe on page 154)

About 10 lasagne pancakes (see recipe on page 155)

250 ml double cream

150 g grated cheese

TOPPING

20 g grated cheese

½–1 tsp dried oregano – optional

25 x 16 cm lasagne dish

Oven temperature
180°C/350°F/Gas 4

SAMOSAS

I used to love samosas. These are close enough to the regular ones to satisfy. Don't be put off by the length of the recipe. Makes 12 pieces.

FILLING

1 tblsp ghee or oil

6 spring onions – chopped, including good portion of green

2 cloves garlic – chopped

1 small hot chilli (or to taste) – finely chopped

1–2 large mild green chillies – chopped

250 g minced lamb

2–3 tsp lemon juice

Salt to taste

PASTRY

6 cooked basic pancakes, about 20 cm diameter, only lightly cooked and pliable (see recipe on page 120)

3 tblsp ground almonds mixed to a thin paste with beaten egg

2 tblsp melted ghee

Rimmed baking tray

*Oven temperature
230°C/450°F/Gas 8*

TO MAKE THE FILLING: Heat the ghee in a saucepan, add the spring onions and garlic and cook for 3–4 minutes. Add the chillies and cook another 2 minutes. Add the meat, stir until browned, then stir in the lemon juice and salt. Cook uncovered for about 30 minutes, stirring occasionally. It needs to be quite dry so don't add any water unless absolutely necessary. Use a slotted spoon to transfer the mixture to a clean bowl, discarding any fat in the pan. Check the seasoning and allow to cool a little before using.

TO MAKE THE SAMOSAS: Cut each pancake in half. Turn the pieces so that the outside edge of the pancake is towards you, cut edge away from you. Put a small spoonful of filling in the centre third of the pancake in a triangle shape.

Spread a little of the ground almond paste on the long cut edge and down each side of the pancake almost to the filling. Fold about 1½ cm of the lower edge up over the filling, then fold the right-hand triangle of pancake over the filling – it doesn't need to cover it completely – then fold the left-hand triangle over the top. Seal the edges well. Turn the samosa over and trim off the ragged edge at the bottom to neaten, making sure the bottom folded edge is holding the filling inside.

Brush each samosa generously all over with melted ghee. (The samosas may be prepared earlier in the day to this point, placed on non-stick baking parchment and chilled until needed. Remove from the parchment before baking).

To cook, place the samosas on a rimmed baking tray – a Swiss-roll tin works well – and bake in a pre-heated oven for about 10–15 minutes until the samosas are a nice brown, turning once or twice. Drain on kitchen paper. Serve warm.

TURKEY ESCALOPES WITH CHEESE SAUCE

4 turkey breast steaks

60 g ground almonds

Pinch of salt

1 egg – beaten

3–4 tblsp ghee or oil

SAUCE

120 ml white wine

140 ml double cream

100 g cheddar-type cheese
– grated

Serves 4.

Spread a sheet of all-purpose food wrap on the worktop and put one turkey breast on top. Cover with another piece of food wrap. Using a rolling pin beat the turkey out to a thin escalope. Repeat with the others.

Put the ground almonds into a shallow dish and add the salt.

Put the egg into a shallow dish. Dip each escalope in the beaten egg and then into the ground almonds to coat lightly.

Heat half the ghee or oil in a frying pan and cook two of the escalopes for 3–4 minutes each side until browned and cooked through so that no pink remains in the middle. Put in a warm oven. Add the remaining ghee or oil to the pan and cook the remaining escalopes. Keep warm while you make the sauce.

TO MAKE THE SAUCE: Pour the wine into the pan and heat, stirring well to get all the juices. Add the cream and bring to the boil. Add the cheese, stirring until melted. Strain into a clean pan, adjust seasoning, heat and serve poured over the escalopes.

SESAME CHEESE BISCUITS

These are delicious to serve with drinks or eat as a snack. Very quick to make. Makes 20–24.

Put butter, cheese, salt and ground almonds into a mixing bowl and mix all together until a dough is formed. Using your hands roll into 20–24 small balls.

Put a few tablespoons of sesame seeds into a bowl and roll each ball in the seeds until coated.

Place them well spaced apart on the baking trays, as the mixture spreads a bit while baking, and flatten each into a neat biscuit shape.

Bake in a pre-heated oven for 10 minutes, turning the trays if necessary to ensure even browning.

Leave to cool slightly on the baking sheets and then transfer to cooling racks until cold and crisp.

100 g soft butter

100 g cheddar cheese – grated

Pinch of salt

120 g ground almonds

Sesame seeds

Non-stick baking trays

Oven temperature 220°C/425°F/Gas 7

BASIC RECIPES

This chapter really speaks for itself. Here you will find both the sweet and cheese pastries that are the base for the flans and quiches, all of which are easy to make and roll. I've included a delicious and easy recipe for Mincemeat, which uses eating apples in place of cooking apples – I find the latter indigestible, possibly because of the starch in them. There are also recipes for a few easy-to-make sauces as so many ready-made sauces contain flour or other starch to thicken them. And if you would like to try making your own Candied Peel have a look at the recipe in this chapter. It's very easy and economical, glucose-syrup free, and uses a part of the fruit that is normally discarded.

I couldn't eat another thing …

SWEET PASTRY FLAN CASE

115 g ground almonds

15 g sifted icing sugar

40 g unsalted butter

Loose-based flan rings of chosen size, greased and base-lined

Oven temperature 170°C/325°F/Gas 3

Makes sufficient to line one 20 cm flan ring or four 9 cm flan rings. The method below is for smaller flans. If making one larger one bake for a few minutes more, if necessary, to cook through and brown.

Mix the ground almonds and icing sugar in a large bowl. Add the butter and rub in until the mix resembles breadcrumbs. Knead lightly until the mix forms a ball of dough without becoming sticky.

Divide the dough into four. Place a piece of all-purpose food wrap on the worktop, put a ball of dough on top and cover with a piece of baking parchment or greaseproof paper. Roll out until large enough to line a flan ring, keeping the dough an even thickness.

Peel off the top layer of paper – this can be used for each one – and lift the dough on the food wrap, and turn over into the tin. Carefully ease the dough into the tin and peel off the food wrap. Neaten the dough in the tin if necessary and trim the edges level. Lightly prick the base with a fork.

Bake in a pre-heated oven for about 12–15 minutes until lightly browned. If the base of the pastry puffs up a little, gently press back into place while still warm. Cool in tins, and then carefully lower the flan rings leaving the pastry on the base.

USES: Best filled just before serving.

Fill with lemon curd and top with grated chocolate.

Fill with grain-free and starch-free chocolate spread to make chocolate tarts.

Fill with sweetened soft cheese mixed with grated lemon rind. Top with fruit and sprinkle with a little icing sugar.

CHEESE PASTRY FLAN CASE

Makes one 23 cm pastry flan case.

Rub the butter into the almonds until the mix is like fine breadcrumbs. Stir in the cheese and knead lightly until the mix forms a dough.

Place a piece of all-purpose food wrap on the worktop, place the dough ball on top and then cover it with a piece of baking parchment or greaseproof paper.

Roll the dough out between the food wrap and paper until large enough to line the tin. Peel off the top paper and lift the pastry on the food wrap. Upturn into the prepared tin and ease into the base and up the sides. Peel off the food wrap and ease any remaining pieces into place. Trim the edges neatly. Lightly prick the base with a fork.

Bake in a pre-heated oven for 12–15 minutes until lightly browned and just cooked through. There is no need to line the pastry with anything – the pastry stays where it's put. If the base rises up a little during baking, gently press it down as soon as it's out of the oven. Leave in the flan ring and fill as directed in the recipe.

NOTE: This quantity can be used to line 4 x 9 cm individual flan tins.

40 g unsalted butter

110 g ground almonds

40 g finely grated cheddar-type cheese

23 cm loose-based flan tin, well greased and base-lined

Oven temperature 170°C/325°F/Gas 3

MINCEMEAT

2 medium eating apples
(about 225 g)

100 g blanched almonds

200 g sultanas

200 g raisins

200 g currants

Grated rind of 2 lemons

Grated rind of 2 oranges

200 g soft brown sugar

6 tblsp brandy

4 tblsp lemon juice

100 g unsalted butter –
melted

Once you've tried home-made mincemeat you'll be hooked. I always use eating apples, as cooking apples don't agree with me. If you don't need to worry, use either. Makes 4 x 350 g jars.

Coarsely mince the apples, the almonds and **half** the sultanas and raisins. Or chop the sultanas, raisins and almonds and grate the apple. Add all the remaining ingredients, adding the butter last and leaving as much sediment behind as possible. Stir very well to mix thoroughly.

Put into a glass or china bowl, cover with food wrap and leave for a day, stirring occasionally. Pack into clean jars, cover tightly and leave in a cool place for a week or two before using.

VANILLA CUSTARD

Serves 4 as an accompanying sauce. See Old-fashioned Sherry Trifle for the double boiler method which takes longer but reduces the risk of curdling.

Combine the egg yolks and the sugar in a bowl, and whisk until pale and mousse like.

Heat the milk until just boiling. Pour slowly onto the yolks, stirring all the time. Strain the custard into a clean, heavy-based pan.

Cook over a gentle heat, stirring all the time to keep the mixture off the bottom of the pan, until it just coats the back of the spoon in a thin film. If using a sugar thermometer the maximum temperature is 74°C/165°F.

NOTE: If the custard overheats it may curdle and will then appear to be slightly scrambled.

Remove from the heat, stir for a few seconds to cool slightly and then add the vanilla essence.

If to be kept warm, cover the pan and place over another containing barely simmering water. Do not let the water touch the bottom of the pan of custard. Stir well before serving in a warmed jug.

3 egg yolks

1½–2 tblsp caster sugar

300 ml full cream milk

½ tsp vanilla essence

Heavy based pan

A sugar thermometer is helpful but not essential

MEAT SAUCE FOR LASAGNE

2 tblsp olive oil

500 g minced lamb

100 g bacon lardons

2 onions – finely chopped

3 cloves garlic – crushed

1 heaped tsp mixed dried herbs

2 x 400 g tins tomatoes

4 heaped tsp tomato purée

6 sun-dried tomatoes – cut into pieces

150 ml wine – red or white

75 g button mushrooms – sliced

Salt to taste

Heat the oil in a large saucepan. Add the lamb and stir until browned. Add the bacon lardons and the onions and fry for a few minutes.

Add the garlic and herbs, season lightly and stir well. Add remaining ingredients and stir well. Bring to the boil and then reduce the heat so the mixture barely simmers.

Cover the pan and cook for 1½ hours, stirring occasionally. If necessary remove the lid for the last 20–30 minutes to allow liquid to reduce. The sauce needs to be quite thick or the lasagne will be too soft to serve neatly. Adjust seasoning.

Use as directed in recipe.

If preferred the wine can be replaced by 150 ml fresh home-made chicken stock.

VARIATION: Rich tomato sauce. Omit the lamb and the bacon lardons. Increase the tomato purée to 6 heaped teaspoons and use 150 g mushrooms and 3 onions.

LASAGNE PANCAKES

This gives a slightly thicker pancake, ideal as 'pasta' for lasagne or for making chicken salad 'wraps'. Makes about 10 pancakes.

Mix the eggs with the water in a mixing jug, add the ground almonds and stir together using a wire whisk. Do not use an electric mixer or a blender.

Heat a non-stick frying pan over a medium heat. Add a very little oil to lightly coat the base of the pan.

Stir the mix well before each pouring. Pour the batter into the pan, using about 35 ml per pancake, tilting pan to make an even pancake shape. The back of a spoon may be used to shape the mixture into a neat square or rectangle to fit the lasagne dish better. Cook until set on top and only lightly browned on the underside. Turn using a spatula and cook until very lightly browned. Stack on a plate as they are cooked. If the pancake tears while turning, spoon a little mix into the tear and it will cook and seal.

NOTE: To use these pancakes as wraps for chicken salad or other snack-in-the-hand-style meals, (see photograph on page 148), cook the pancakes a little longer until browned and of a nice appearance.

4 eggs

160 ml cold water

70 g sifted ground almonds

A little olive oil

CANDIED PEEL

1 grapefruit

3 oranges

4 lemons

750 g granulated sugar

This is very easy to make. I use the following proportions to make a little over 400 g of candied peel, but vary the proportions to suit your taste, or make just one type. Choose fruit with a nice thick skin.

Wash the fruit well. Cut the lemons in half and squeeze out the juice. Cut the rinds in half again. Cut the oranges and grapefruit in half. Scoop out the flesh and use for fruit salads. Cut the rinds in half again.

Put the grapefruit peel in one saucepan and just cover with water. Put the orange and lemon peel in another pan and cover with water. Bring to the boil, reduce heat, cover and cook gently for 1–1½ hours until tender. If using grapefruit change the water a couple of times.

Drain the grapefruit, discarding the cooking water. Drain the orange and lemon peel, reserving the liquid. Make it up to 500 ml with water if necessary. Put the liquid into a pan and add 500 g of the sugar. Dissolve the sugar over a low heat, bring to the boil and then remove from the heat. Put all the peels into the sugar solution, stir well, cover and leave in a cool place for two days.

Strain the peel, reserving the syrup. Put the syrup and the remaining 250 g of sugar back into the pan and dissolve over a low heat. Add the peel and simmer gently for 50–60 minutes until semi-transparent. Remove from the heat and leave the peel in the syrup, in a cool place, for up to 2 weeks depending on how sweet you would like the peel to be.

Drain off the syrup and place the peel on wire racks over baking trays and leave in a warm place until dry. If preferred put in a very low oven for 2–3 hours to dry but take care not to let it harden. Roll in caster sugar to coat and then store in an airtight jar until required. Cut into strips or dice to use.

VARIATION: To serve as an after-dinner treat cut into strips, roll in caster sugar to coat and dip the ends in melted dark chocolate. Leave on non-stick paper to dry.

CRANBERRY & CLEMENTINE SAUCE

Makes about 650 ml to serve 8–10.

Put the cranberries into a saucepan. Remove any stalk remains from the clementines, cut in half and slice thinly. Add to the pan with 150 ml water. Bring to the boil and cook gently for about 10 minutes until the cranberries have burst. Add the sugar and port and stir over a gentle heat for 5–10 minutes until the sauce has thickened.

Serve warm or cold with baked ham or poultry.

250 g fresh cranberries

2–3 clementines – well washed

100 g soft brown sugar

4 tblsp port

STARCH-FREE FRENCH DRESSING

Serves 3–4.

Place all the ingredients together in a small jug. Mix well with a fork and leave to stand for about 10 minutes to allow the flavours to blend. Adjust seasoning if necessary. Stir well before serving.

60 ml olive oil

1 tblsp cider vinegar – or to taste

¼ tsp salt – or to taste

1 tsp dried salad herbs

BARBECUE SAUCE

Serves 4–6.

Chop the onions quite small. Melt the butter in a pan, add the onions and cook over a medium heat for 5–10 minutes until softened.

Mix all the rest of the ingredients to a smooth cream. Stir into the onion mixture and bring to the boil and simmer for 10–15 minutes until the sauce has thickened. Adjust seasoning if necessary.

A good pinch of mixed dried herbs may be added.

Serve with burgers in buns, chops or baked chicken.

2 medium onions

60 g butter

120 ml water

2 tblsp cider or wine vinegar

3 tblsp dark brown sugar

2–3 tsp starch-free wholegrain mustard

2–3 tblsp tomato purée

Salt to taste

INDEX

Almond biscuits 90
Almond cup cakes 39
Almond rocks 75
Apple parcels 104-5
Apples 11
Asparagus cheese pancakes 124
Asparagus & smoked trout flan 131
Bacon brunch pancakes 125
Bacon & leek flan 136
Baked chicken nuggets 138
Baked syrup sponges 107
Baking parchment 9, 13
Baking powder 10
Baking tins 9, 13
Baps sesame 22
Barbecue sauce 157
Bars
  date bars 70
  millionaires' shortbread 76-7
  walnut brownies 91
Basic bread 15, 16
Basic pancakes 120
Basic recipes 148-57
Battenburg cake 48-9
Biscotti 26
Biscuits 68-91
  almond biscuits 90
  almond rocks 75
  brandy snaps 80-1
  choc-chip cookies 73
  chocolate orange drops 74
  coconut biscuits 71
  double choc-chip cookies 89
  Easter biscuits 82
  ginger biscuit people 72
  hazelnut biscuits 78
  lemon thins 88
  macadamia & white chocolate cookies 79
  mini choc-chip meringues 83
  piped chocolate biscuits 85
  piped vanilla biscuits 84
  sesame cheese biscuits 147
  vanilla hearts 86-7
Black olive & feta cheese bread 20
Black pepper 11
Blueberries 11
Blueberry cheesecakes 114
Blueberry hearts 66
Brandy snaps 80-1
Bread 14-29
  basic 16
  black olive & feta cheese 20
  cheese & onion 19

cheese & pinenut rolls 21
Christmas breads 24
date & walnut swirl 25
herb 18
kougelhopf 28-29
pecan danish 27
sesame baps 22
storing and freezing 11
sultana & poppy-seed 26
sun-dried tomato & rosemary 17
sweet rolls 29
toasted tea cakes 23
Brownies, walnut 91
Burgers 22
Butter 11
Butter cream, raspberry 44
Buying ingredients 8, 10, 11
Cake decorations 10
Cakes 30-67
  Battenburg cake 48-9
  blueberry hearts 66
  chocolate cup cakes 47
  chocolate squares 56
  chocolate & hazelnut torte 61
  chocolate layer cake 32
  chocolate & raspberry butter cream cake 44
  chocolate sponge fingers 40
  chocolate Swiss roll 38
  Christmas cake 54-5
  coconut madeleines 33
  coconut picnic slice 41
  coffee & walnut layer cake 35
  Easter nests 65
  French fancies 42-3
  French madeleines 34
  fruit cake 36-7
  iced sponge 67
  iced vanilla cup cakes 39
  layered lemon squares 51
  mini chocolate kougelhopfs 60
  mocha buns 64
  orange ring cake 50
  sachertorte 52-3
  simnel cake 58-9
  sponge fingers 57
  Swiss roll 46
  Yule log 62-3
Candied peel 156
Caramel 77
Cheese 11
  asparagus cheese pancakes 124
  black olive & feta cheese bread 20
  blueberry cheesecakes 114

cheese & bacon quiches 132-3
cheese blintzes 115
cheese & onion bread 19
cheese & pinenut rolls 21
cheese sauce 146
cheese tartlets 134
continental cheesecake 100-1
lasagne 142-3
light cheese pudding 137
sesame cheese biscuits 147
Cheese & bacon quiches 132-3
Cheese blintzes 115
Cheese & onion bread 19
Cheese pastry flan cases 151
Cheese & pine nut rolls 21
Cheese sauce 146
Cheese tartlets 134
Cheesecakes
  blueberry cheesecakes 114
  continental cheesecake 100-1
Cherries 11
Chicken
  baked chicken nuggets 138
  chicken dippers 139
Chicken dippers 139
Choc-chip cookies 73
Chocolate
  buying 10
  choc-chip cookies 73
  chocolate cup cakes 47
  chocolate squares 56
  chocolate fudge walnut tarts 96
  chocolate & hazelnut torte 61
  chocolate layer cake 32
  chocolate leaves 44
  chocolate orange drops 74
  chocolate pancakes with chocolate sauce 121
  chocolate & raspberry butter cream cake 44
  chocolate sponge fingers 40
  chocolate Swiss roll 38
  chocolate waffles 127
  double choc-chip cookies 89
  macadamia & white chocolate cookies 79
  melting 10-11
  mini choc-chip meringues 83
  mini kougelhopfs 60
  piped chocolate biscuits 85
  sachertorte 52-3
Chocolate cup cakes 47
Chocolate squares 56
Chocolate fudge walnut tarts 96

Chocolate & hazelnut torte 61
Chocolate layer cake 32
Chocolate leaves 44
Chocolate orange drops 74
Chocolate pancakes with chocolate sauce 121
Chocolate & raspberry butter cream cake 44
Chocolate sauce
  chocolate pancakes 121
  chocolate waffles 127
Chocolate sponge fingers 40
Chocolate swiss roll 38
Chocolate waffles 127
Christmas breads 24
Christmas cake 54-5
Christmas pudding 116
Coconut biscuits 71
Coconut madeleines 33
Coconut picnic slice 41
Coffee & walnut layer cake 35
Continental cheesecake 100-1
Conversion tables 160
Cooking apples 11
Cranberries 11
Cranberry & clementine sauce 157
Crêpes suzette 122
Cup cakes
  almond 39
  chocolate 47
  iced vanilla 39
Currant & hazelnut kougelhopf 29
Custard 109, 153
Danish pastry 27
Date bars 70
Date & walnut swirl 25
Desserts 92-117
Double choc-chip cookies 89
Easter biscuits 82
Easter nests 65
Eggs
  adding egg yolks 10
  size 9
  whisking egg whites 10
Equipment 13
Fan assisted ovens 8
Fish fingers 140
Flans 128-47
  asparagus & smoked trout flan 131
  bacon & leek flan 136
  cheese & bacon quiches 132-3
  cheese pastry flan case 151
  French onion tart 130
  raspberry & strawberry sponge flan 106
  spinach & mushroom flan 135
  sweet pastry flan case 150

see also Tarts
Folding in 10
Food wrap 9
Freezing 11
French dressing 157
French fancies 42-3
French madeleines 34
French onion tart 130
Fruit cake 36-7
Fruit tarts 94-5
Ghee 11
Ginger biscuit people 72
Glacé cherries 11
Glucose syrup 8, 11
Greasing tins 9
Ground almonds 10
Hazelnut biscuits 78
Herb bread 18
Iced sponge 67
Iced vanilla cup cakes 39
Icing sugar 10
Jam tarts 97
Kougelhopf 28
  currant & hazlenut kougelhopf 29
  mini chocolate kougelhopfs 60
Lasagne
  meat lasagne 143, 154
  pancakes 155
  spinach & cheese lasagne 142
Layered lemon squares 51
Lemon meringue pies 103
Lemon tart 99
Lemon thins 88
Light cheese pudding 137
Lining tins 9
Macadamia & white chocolate cookies 79
Madeleines
  coconut 33
  French 34
Marzipan 11, 55
  Battenburg cake 48
  French fancies 42
  simnel cake 58
Meat lasagne 143
Melting chocolate 10-11
Meringues
  almond rocks 75
  lemon meringue pies 103
  mini choc-chip 83
Millionaires' shortbread 76-7
Mince pies 102
Mincemeat 152
Mini choc-chip meringues 83
Mini chocolate kougelhopfs 60
Mixers 13
Mocha buns 64

Old-fashioned sherry trifle 108-9
Olive bread 20
Orange ring cake 50
Oven temperatures 8
Pancakes 118-27
  apple parcels 104-5
  asparagus cheese pancakes 124
  bacon brunch pancakes 125
  basic 120
  cheese blintzes 115
  chocolate pancakes with chocolate sauce 121
  crêpes suzette 122
  for lasagne 155
  for salad wraps 155
  scotch pancakes 123
Pastry 150-1
Pecan danish 27
Pecan maple pie 98
Picnic pizza 141
Pies
  apple parcels 104-5
  lemon meringue pies 103
  mince pies 102
Pineapple upside down 110
Piped chocolate biscuits 85
Piped vanilla biscuits 84
Pizza 141
Poppy-seed bread
  baps 22
  basic bread 16
  sultana & poppy seed bread 26
Quiches 132-3
Raspberry & strawberry sponge flan 106
Rolls
  cheese & pinenut rolls 21
  sweet 29
Sachertorte 52-3
Samosas 144-5
Sauces 157
Savouries 128-47
Scales 13
Scotch pancakes 123
Sesame baps 22
Sesame cheese biscuits 147
Sesame seed bread 16
Sherry trifle 108-9
Shortcake, strawberry 112-13
Simnel cake 58-9
Spices 11
Spinach & cheese lasagne 142
Spinach & mushroom flan 135
Sponge fingers 57
  chocolate 40
Spoon sizes 9

Starch 8
  in ingredients 10, 11
Starch free French dressing 157
Strawberry & apple crumble 111
Strawberry shortcake 112-13
Sultana & poppy seed bread 26
Sun-dried tomato & rosemary bread 17
Sweet pastries 92-117
Sweet pastry flan case 150
Sweet rolls 29

Swiss roll 46
Tarts
  cheese tartlets 134
  chocolate fudge walnut tarts 96
  individual fruit tarts 94-5
  jam tarts 97
  lemon tart 99
  pecan maple pie 98
  see also Flans
Tea cakes 23
Tiramisu 117
Toast 16

Toasted tea cakes 23
Tomato bread 17
Trifle 108-9
Turkey escalopes with cheese sauce 146
Vanilla custard 153
Vanilla hearts 86-7
Waffles 126
  chocolate waffles 127
Walnut brownies 91
Whisking egg whites 10
Wraps 155
Yule log 62-3

CONVERSION CHARTS

Oven Temperatures

°C	°F	Gas Mark
100	200	$1/4$
110	225	$1/4$
130	250	$1/2$
140	275	1
150	300	2
170	325	3
180	350	4
190	375	5
200	400	6
220	425	7
230	450	8
240	475	9

Weights

Ounces	Grams
1	30
2	55
3	85
4 ($1/4$ lb)	115
5	140
6	170
7	200
8 ($1/2$ lb)	225
9	255
10	285
11	310
12 ($3/4$ lb)	340
13	370
14	400
15	425
16 (1lb)	455

Volumes

Fluid ounces	Millilitres
1	30
2	55
3	85
4	115
5 ($1/4$ pt)	140
6	170
7	200
8	225
9	255
10 ($1/2$ pt)	285
11	310
12	340
13	370
14	400
15 ($3/4$pt)	425
16	455
17	485
18	510
19	540
20 (1pt)	570